THE
INSIDER
BUYOUT

By Donald R. Dubendorf and M. John Storey

 Storey Communications, Inc.
Pownal, VT 05261

Printed in the United States by R. R. Donnelley
First Printing, September, 1985

Library of Congress Cataloging-in-Publication Data

Dubendorf, Donald R.
   The insider buyout.

   1. Management buyouts — United States. I. Storey,
M. John, 1943-   . II. Title.
HD2746.5.D83   1985   658.1'6   84-52258
ISBN 0-88266-387-9

Contents

Introduction

This book tells how you, the manager of a business division, can create the opportunity of your lifetime with a proven technique we call the "insider buyout."

We tell you how you can buy the business you now manage.

We share with you the lessons we learned from the insider buyout of a small publishing company so that you can profit from them.

And we highlight the personal stories of several dozen other insider buyouts, as told by successful managers-turned-entrepreneurs.

There is a message here, too, for heads of corporations large and small who find themselves saddled with divisions that don't fit into the corporate plans for the future or that are losing money. Can an insider buyout free them of this headache without damage to the personnel of that division? Can this be done without rancor and at little cost (and possibly great profit) to the corporation?

This is a good-news book, a how-to-do-it book. This is not a history, critique, or technical manual. It is not a book about the megadeals you've been reading about every day. Our emphasis is on the success of professional managers, not on the rewards of professional investors.

Our mission in *The Insider Buyout* is to explain how you, a middle or senior manager, can turn even the most dismal of employment situations into a golden opportunity for both you and your corporation. Our case histories offer insights into the thinking of successful managers. These will be especially valuable to you, the middle manager, and to corporate heads, lawyers, accountants, lenders, and the families of those managers who are planning insider buyouts.

Our insider buyout technique is primarily geared for the most popular type of management buyout, and that is the purchase of all or part of the assets of a small to medium-sized division by one or more managers. These assets could be the corporate division you are now managing, or they could be the rights to a software program, a line of microscopes, a storage warehouse, a mail order department, a small manufacturing corporation, a chain of restaurants, or something even larger.

Our book is more about Main Street than about Wall Street. However, many aspects of our insider buyout technique have also been used in some of the largest and most publicized management buyouts, the leveraged purchases by groups of outside investors with the involvement of managers.

We have added to our personal experiences by researching hundreds of recent management buyouts and pursuing more than 100 of the best of these through correspondence and interviews. This has been valuable to us. We found common threads among the techniques of managers who had performed successful insider buyouts, techniques that seemed to know no boundaries of region, size, or experience.

We will share these common threads with you.

We will tell you how they did it.

The Authors and Their Story

This was a small town, small numbers deal. In other words, an average deal.

We live in northwestern Massachusetts, in the foothills of the Berkshire Mountains near the New York and Vermont borders. Our homes are in Williamstown, near Williams College, one of the finest locations in the world to live and raise a family.

This was a key factor when we considered buying out the publishing division from Garden Way, Inc., in early 1983. John wanted to fit his work more closely into his life, not change his life to follow job or career opportunities elsewhere for someone else's convenience. He was determined to create his own opportunities.

John grew up outside New York City, was graduated from Williams, worked for ten years in New York publishing houses (Time, Inc., and Hearst), then found an opportunity to settle in the country—Williamstown—by accepting a position in nearby Troy, New York, with Garden Way, Inc., makers of the Troy-Bilt RotoTiller.

Don grew up in dairy country in upstate New York, and he also was graduated from Williams, and then from Boston University Law School. But, instead of trying Boston or New York after graduation, he moved immediately to Williamstown to practice law.

We had not known each other in college, but shared a common appreciation for life in a small New England college town. So when John began looking for an attorney who shared his personal and business orientation, we hit it off almost immediately.

During the 1970s, Garden Way, Inc. had grown, and diversified rapidly into a wide range of gardening and homesteading products. One of its subsidiaries was a publishing division in Charlotte, Vermont, a three-hour drive north from Williamstown. Following a major corporate restructuring, Garden Way, Inc. gave John the job of directing the publishing and other divisions in Charlotte.

Soon he was called upon for recommendations for the future of the publishing division, the business he loved and where he felt most at home. Publishing really didn't fit with the remainder of the privately held manufacturing and marketing corporation. More personally, he had to decide what to do with his home in Williamstown, a town he loved, and he had to plan for his future beyond Garden Way, Inc.—a company he loved—if the publishing and other divisions in Charlotte were sold or liquidated.

He talked openly about these life decisions with his wife, Martha, and with Don and several other close advisors.

All of this led to development of plans for our insider buyout — but only after a long and exhilarating process of examining the alternatives. "That examination was a matter of doing our homework," said Don. "That was the key. And the decisions that we eventually made were made together. We found this, too, to be key."

The result was that after strategy sessions and meetings with supportive corporate officials, all agreed that everyone's best interests—ours and theirs—were served if the corporation approved a sale of the publishing company assets to us—a new corporation, Storey Communications, Inc.

The buyout techniques we used require a hell of a lot of hard work—and some skills. But you don't have to have all the skills. Persons who have them and who will work with you can be found in your home town. Virtually everyone else we talked with felt the same way.

Victor Kiam, who bought Remington, made this point come alive for us. When we asked him to whom small-town managers should first go for advice when they were thinking about an insider buyout, we expected him to recommend New York brokers, law firms, or venture capitalists.

"Go to your local bank," Kiam said. "Seek out the people in the community who are the leaders. I'd call the president of the largest department store, because he's involved in real estate deals every month for his stores and is usually tied in with the leaders. Say what you want to find out and you will find these people very gracious."

Good counsel. And, like many other aspects of the IBO technique, simple, straightforward, direct.

Our Contributors

Our original method in writing this book was to use the techniques we developed in preparing our insider buyout plans. We would pass notes back and forth among ourselves and our associates, and then sit down and argue over the fine points. (You'll notice that we say "we" most of the time. In some cases, we say "I." That's John discussing parts of the venture in which he alone was involved.)

Then we began testing our recommendations with a few who had made successful acquisitions, such as Victor Kiam of Remington and Bill Farley of Farley Industries. They were immediately helpful.

From them we found that the managers of both small and large insider buyouts had stories to tell that had not been told previously, and that these stories would assist those considering a similar move.

The result is that this book is a combination of the lessons we learned in one insider buyout compared with the experiences of many others involved in similar deals, some smaller than ours, some much larger.

Our goal remained unchanged, however. We wanted to tell you, a middle-to-senior level manager, how to assess your chances for negotiating an insider buyout, and how to proceed if your chances look good.

We'd like to emphasize two themes right now, and we'll come back to them again so that you will keep them in the front of your mind.

One is how to realize many of your life's goals through personal independence. In effect, you can improve the quality of your life because of the workplace, not in spite of it. One way to do this is to gain control of your division or your piece of your employer's business in an insider buyout.

This theme is linked directly to another. That's *how to develop business and personal relationships that will aid you in your buyout.*

Remember these themes as we start the book with an explanation of the insider buyout and how it works, and how it is suited to many who find themselves stymied, through no particular fault of their own, by their position within a corporation.

Chapter I

You and the Insider Buyout

You're a key company executive, a profit manager, a senior operations manager of a corporate division. You may be a stockholder, too, and perhaps a corporate official.

You're competent. You're trusted. You have vision. And you have gotten where you are because you have a track record of finding creative, effective solutions to tough problems.

You are still growing and you're hungering for new challenges and responsibilities. But your primary job lately has been to carry the torch for your division at corporate headquarters and to boost flagging morale back on the front. Because, through no fault of your own, you're head of a sagging part of the corporation, a "bleeder," the division that doesn't quite fit.

Because "success has many fathers, and failure is a bastard," meetings at headquarters have become an embarrassment and even a waste of time rather than a source of vital support for the division.

You sense that headquarters views you as the constant bearer of bad tidings. It's been a long time since anyone at headquarters has said, "Good job."

Your learning curve has flattened out. Perhaps you deliver precise data to headquarters, but it becomes fuzzy when consolidated with other corporate activities.

Your fast-track career has been sidetracked. You have reached a plateau and you're in a vulnerable position.

You are caught in the middle. Not only vertically between your bosses and your division employees, but horizontally between staff advisors and other operating division managers — your peers.

You feel a genuine loss of control. You feel restricted in your management efforts to a greater degree than is personally acceptable. Instead of managing change within a system, change and the system are managing you.

And it is that system that is slowly killing your enthusiasm and motivation. For the first time since your college years, you have caught yourself looking forward to lunch when you aren't even hungry.

"It really hit me one day when I was in Boston making a speech about Garden Way's growth to the New England Direct Marketing Club," says John. "I had a drink with Alan Lewis, who had just left a top job at Trans National in Boston to form his own company.

" 'I recommend it,' said Alan. 'The highs will be higher and the lows lower. You'll love it.' "

When you sense that you've grown restless within the corporate environment, it's time to reexamine things. Perhaps you are increasingly having to make compromises between your personal goals and the needs of the corporation.

You have probably caught yourself dreaming of running an inn in Vermont. A cattle ranch in Idaho. Even staying home, writing a book and raising sheep in the back yard.

You feel your security with the corporation is being threatened. You are facing a career watershed — opportunity and peril on one side, stagnation on the other. You are uneasy and undecided. But you are still ambitious, still growing, and still ready to lead.

You are ready for some dynamic changes in your life.

You hunger for new management challenges. More business adventures. You are ready to get going, even if it means going it alone.

Choosing Your Alternatives

You are not desperate for a job. You could walk away from your current job and find something else worth doing. You have options, alternatives. You are desperate — not for a job — but for a way to

use your management talents and creativity in a fulfilling vocation.
What are your options? Let's break the situation down into manageable chunks.

Do Nothing

You could change nothing. Stick it out with the corporation. Reassert your management skills and hope to set some fires at headquarters. But isn't this what you've been trying all along? You could give it your best and your misfit division would probably still be misfit. Your bosses might agree to some compromises, but compromises may fall short. Staying put guarantees you'll be part of the problem with no assurance you'll be part of the solution.

Retire

You could retire. But let's get serious, you're too young and ambitious with too much skill and experience as a manager for that option.

Buy a Business

You could buy a country inn or ranch. That would keep you physically and intellectually active in many ways and be fun for your kids. But for the purposes of your corporate management career as discussed in this book, such a drastic career and lifestyle change would be tantamount to retirement.

Be a Consultant

You could resign, order some stationery and business cards, send out some letters, open an office, and become a consultant. You have the wisdom, experience, and contacts to succeed in this field.

But for someone who has grown to love being involved in the perks, power, and decision-making of the business world, this could prove a thoroughly unsatisfying way to spend the prime of your life.

Find Another Job

You could find a good job with another corporation, perhaps a competitor. But what evidence do you see that a new corporation is going to be any different than the one you're with?

A Better Alternative

We think there's a better alternative. Buy your division from your corporation and begin to run the business your own way. We call that an insider buyout.

Managing an insider buyout may not have been an option that you had considered before picking up this book.

There is a myth that a leveraged buyout, even a small insider's leveraged buyout, is a farfetched and complicated transaction. You might have believed that such a deal would be beyond your reach — especially if highly leveraged, by which we mean using the assets of the corporation as collateral, borrowing against them, and paying off the loan with future corporate earnings.

It is the purpose of this book to demystify and dispel that myth, the myth that a leveraged buyout, even a highly leveraged buyout, is the exclusive province of a Texaco or a Standard Oil of California in partnership with one or more Wall Street investment firms.

Consider an insider buyout. For your situation it could be the key to your future, the vehicle to help you reach those elusive personal and professional goals. Let's explore it. But first, a quick look at yourself.

A LOOK AT YOURSELF

Answer the following questions and you may get some idea of whether you and your position in the corporate world are right for an insider buyout.

1. Are you the manager of an underproductive, under-achieving, backwater product, division, or program?

2. Does your division fail to fit with the rest of your company?

3. Do you have plans for your product, division, or program that could turn it around?

4. Have these plans been presented, but rejected by your superiors, possibly for reasons not closely related to the problems you have confronted?

5. Are your opportunities for advancement in the corporate hierarchy limited because you have been closely identified with your division in the eyes of your superior?

6. Are you growing restless in the corporate environment — the meetings, the compromise of personal goals?

If you answer yes to questions 1 and 2 and at least one other question, you are the type of person who should read this book with a view toward putting into practice what it offers.

What Is an IBO?

An insider buyout is a friendly management buyout. The following are part of every such transaction:

1. Both the buyer (you, the manager) and the seller (your corporation) are working inside the corporation for the same goals and are faced with the same problems. These trusting parties are eager to complete the deal. Both understand the business and the problems that led to these negotiations. They understand each other. This makes negotiations easier. There is nothing hidden, hostile, upperhanded, or even underhanded in the IBO. In the end, both the buyer and the seller see themselves as winners.

2. You, the person who negotiates the deal and ends up with the new company, are a trusted official of the parent company, an insider, not an outsider trying to profit from a corporate problem. You may have been given the assignment of finding a solution to the corporate problem, found several alternatives, then concluded that the best answer from the corporate standpoint is the insider buyout.

3. The deal is written and managed by you, not by your corporate superiors, not by financiers, not by hired accountants — yours or anyone else's. It is you, the buyer, who initiates and propels an insider buyout and thereby controls the destiny of your division.

4. The buyout is friendly. A cooperative spirit is seen on both sides during negotiations. This means you can expect and should get willing and responsible help from top officials during the negotiations. And it can mean far more than smiles and handshakes when the deal is completed. It can mean a continuing warm relationship between the new company and its corporate parent in such areas as products, sales, and services. Such a continuing relationship resulted from the buyout of Garden Way Publishing.

5. The buyout puts control of the new company directly in your hands. You can try your own methods, not continue using methods that you and possibly the corporate officials saw as losers. The buyout is an opportunity for you to create a better life for yourself.

6. The insider buyout is a way for a public or private company to improve its position by quickly peeling off or selling any part of the company that is suffering from poor productivity, lagging sales, top-heavy costs, a lackluster product range — or all of the above.

Summing up, the key to the insider buyout is that it provides long-term solutions to the diverse problems of the corporation, the division, and you, the manager.

The Insider Buyout Process

The insider buyout process begins with a fundamental personal decision — what you, the manager, want to do with your life. Then you must weigh how the division you manage fits into this picture.

The process focuses on the opportunities and problems of your division, something you are in a better position to assess than anyone else in the world. If your decision is that you could make your division more profitable if you worked on your own and that this move would offer you an opportunity to reach your life goals, your next step is to move toward the buyout.

You will have a dual role in the corporate structure throughout the negotiations, with the many new dangers and opportunities that that creates. There are risks, to be sure, but if you proceed carefully and wisely, you can end negotiations at any stage and return to your role within the corporation.

Business Relationships

We feel that the success of an insider buyout depends less on money and more on human relationships, specifically those you develop with business advisors and those you nurture with existing superiors. Surprising? Our findings from dozens of conversations show that the successful buyouts were those performed by managers with teams of friends and advisors at their sides working within the corporation with close and trusted peers and superiors.

The successful managers of insider buyouts we interviewed said self-sufficiency means gaining control of your own business, while relying on friends and advisors for support and counsel to help you. This reliance is much more than a defensive technique; it's a positive, affirmative move, going on the offensive when there are opportunities to be seized.

Who Needs to Know About IBOs

If you are to manage an insider buyout, you must, of course, understand the principles of the IBO that we've just gone over. A depth of understanding is essential if you are to react quickly and correctly when opportunities arise for you during negotiations. But there are others who need to know the inner workings of this process.

At the top of our list of others we'll put:

1. The corporate strategist and, with him, all others in the corporation involved in the decision-making on this move.

That strategist must see the IBO as a method of dealing with an underproductive division with a minimum of negative publicity. He must see it is a win-win situation for both you and the corporation. He must understand that it is, for the corporation, the best of several alternative moves that have been studied in depth.

2. The personal or business advisors. The attorneys, accountants, and consultants involved in the negotiations must understand their roles in the process of an insider buyout. In particular, your advisors must understand your dual role in the early days of negotiations.

3. The lender. At some point, you will be seeking the funds for financing the IBO. Bankers are comfortable only when working in familiar situations that promise a completed business plan, a proven cash flow, and experienced management. The IBO must appear familiar to them. Present it as no more than a leveraged buyout on a small scale at the local level.

Part of your work as the leader in an IBO will be to acquaint these people with this method of transferring assets from one corporation to another and to explain to them their role in that transfer.

POPULAR TECHNIQUES FOR BUYING CONTROL OF A COMPANY

Deal	Buyer	Buys Target	From Seller	Leveraged Financing
A. Outsiders with help from insiders buying a business from shareholders:				
LBO	Investors & Managers	Shares of Assets of a company	Share-holders	80-100%
B. Insiders buying a business from shareholders:				
Buyback	Board of Directors	Shares of a company	Share-holders	0-100%
Management Buyout	Managers	Shares of a company	Share-holders	0-100%
C. Insiders buying a business from their employers:				
Insider Buyout	Manager	Assets or shares of co/sub/div *	Corp. or share-holders	0-100%
Employee Buyout	Employees	Assets or shares of co/sub/div *	Corp. or share-holders	0-100%

* *(co = company, sub = subsidiary, div = division)*

Chapter II

Profits from the Buyouts

The trend towards more and more corporate mergers — once called the Conglomerate Era — has been reversed.

Conglomeration has turned into deconglomeration.

Diversification has turned into consolidation.

Decentralized super-corporations are being restructured into centralized enterprises.

These trends have combined with the more obvious reasons for selling a business to make this a golden period for a business buyout.

You may be facing the opportunity of a lifetime.

Now is the time to ride with the trends and consider doing an insider buyout of the company or division you manage and establishing your own business.

For you, these trends and techniques could mean trouble—or opportunity.

Regardless of what you decide to do with the rest of your life, it will pay you to study these trends and new investment techniques.

Is there any chance that the division you manage or the corporation that employs you could be put on the market?

Or is there any chance the parent company could become the target of an unfriendly takeover?

In either case, will you stick it out? Or will you be looking for a chance to get out? Would you consider buying in? Or would you consider buying out?

We urge you, the manager, to determine in advance your life's goals and your tolerance for corporate upheaval.

We urge you to add the insider buyout to your menu of career and investment choices.

End of the Conglomerate Era

It is not possible to determine exactly when the Conglomerate Era ended and the Entrepreneurial Era began.

There is no official census of sales of corporations that distinguishes between deals in which corporations grow larger or get smaller.

Buyouts, divestitures, and other corporate contractions are listed in official statistics under "Mergers and Acquisitions" along with the deals by which corporations expand and diversify.

We can spot the trends, however, in the vast assemblage of data from W. T. Grimm & Co., the Chicago merger consultants and publishers.

The number of subsidiaries being split off from major corporations more than doubled between 1980 and 1984.

The private buyouts of large public companies increased steadily from thirteen deals in 1980 to fifty-seven in 1984.

Mergers and acquisitions totaled 4,000 to 6,000 a year in the late 1960s and early 1970s. They dropped to a low of 1,900 in 1980 and have hovered around 2,500 a year since then.

Other sources confirm the deconglomeration movement.

Massachusetts Institute of Technology researcher David Birch reports one-third of the companies on the *Fortune* 500 in 1970 were not on the list in 1981. [1]

And an editor at Moody's Investors Service confirms that authoritative statistics on deconglomeration are unavailable, but he speaks in hushed tones, off the record, about "the unraveling of corporate America."

Corporations speak openly of their reasons for this turnabout. They hope to simplify the corporate structure. By doing this, they can get a clearer vision of the corporate direction, set up uniform measurements of performance for all corporate divisions, and, in the end, improve the performance and thus the profitability of the corporation.

The Conglomerate Cure-all

Diversification by conglomeration was seen as the key to the future by corporate leaders in the thirty years after World War II. Mergers were believed to be the cure for everything from a lack of capital, management expertise, material resources, and product lines to a lack of national advertising, tax shelters, and growth.

In those postwar days, management was thought to be more science than art. The goal was to develop a new breed of professional super-manager. Managers were taught that their skills were universal and transferable from steel mill to soft-drink firm to commodity exporting office to conglomerate headquarters.

The business advice for firms from petroleum companies to dairy farms was get big or get out.

Managers were told of competition, if you can't beat 'em, merge.

It was a matter of corporate policy that inefficiencies within the conglomerate could be solved by a time-and-motion study, a new organizational flow chart, or better trained managers. State-of-the-art corporate controls, planning, and information systems were intended to help America win the peace with the same efficiency it won the war.

Merger advocates developed figures that suggested all the nation's business would be centralized in 200 corporations by 1990. [2] And John Kenneth Galbraith warned the trend would turn America into a dreaded industrial state.

H. Ross Perot, James Joseph Ling, and Bernard Cornfeld were among the brash, young corporate speculators who pioneered with corporate takeovers in the macro-merger, conglomerate era during the Great Society-Vietnam War days of the late 1960s.

The Trend Turns

However, the mergers of unrelated firms peaked in 1968-69 at a time of threatening anti-trust action and changes in accounting standards. This was also a time of some dramatic conglomerate failures.

Ling's conglomerate, Ling-Temco-Vought (LTV), began suffering from cash flow problems in the late 1960s. In 1970 he was forced to resign as LTV began to sell its major acquisitions.

Cornfeld's international mutual fund empire also collapsed in 1970.

And Perot lost a billion dollars in one month that year when Electronic Data System stock lost favor with institutional investors.

Because the number of reported "merger and acquisitions" has increased in recent years to about 2,500 per year from the 1974 low of 1,900, there is frequently talk and headlines about M&As setting new records for the ten-year period.

Let's face it, the 2,500 annual M&As is a far cry from the 6,100 deals that were closed in 1969 at the height of merger mania.

What's more—actually, what's less—the M&A figures are not exclusively for corporate expansion, but are an overall measure of sales of corporations including the increase in divestitures, buyouts, spin-offs, shadeouts, reorganizations, and other corporate contractions.

More than half of the 2,500 deals that W.T. Grimm & Co. tracked in 1983 were leveraged buyouts, meaning the firms were being taken out, not absorbed. [3]

In both 1983 and 1984, more than half of the some 2,500 M&As tracked by Grimm involved private firms, for the most part smaller firms whose securities are closely held or privately traded. [4]

In 1948, when the figures were first kept by the Federal Trade Commission, the nation's 200 largest firms did 100 percent of the major acquisitions—all four of them. That percentage dropped steadily to 23 percent by 1979, the last year for which the figures are available. [5]

Small Deals Important

The Wall Street Journal explained it this way in a December 1983 front page article: "For all the Wall Street rumors about megamergers, it is relatively small deals involving target companies whose shares aren't even traded publicly that account for most of the current jump in merger activity."

Few firms are continuing to operate today on the manage-by-merger system. One exception is American Express Co., which is continuing to build what it hopes will be the prototypical- financial services conglomerate for the twenty-first century. But, based on recent earnings results, it's not altogether clear that this formula is working.

Most other conglomerates have already reversed their field, frequently under new ownership and management, and are changing back to tightly focused operations.

Conglomeration and diversification did not work because people did not fit into the molds that management theorists had cast for them. In many cases, the value of a group of managers proved to be less than the sum of its parts.

Conglomeration was a good theory in the management textbooks, but it ultimately failed the test of human dynamics.

In our own publishing industry, appreciation and understanding of smaller business and renewed entrepreneurship has been reborn. RCA divested Random House. New American Library, under Bob Diforio, did its own management buyout.

Role of the Entrepreneurs

The nation's entrepreneurs are on the march as never before. There are many reasons for this. David C. Allais, president of Intermec Corp., gives one, in an interview with *Business Week.*

"Adapting new technologies to market niches is what the entrepreneur in his garage does best. He can put together a solution faster than a larger, sluggish company that is not so focused."

The trend was hailed by President Reagan in an address to young people: "Why not set out with your friends on the path to adventure and start your own business? You too can become leaders in this great new era of progress — the age of the entrepreneur."

Says Kevin Farrell of *Venture* magazine, "By almost any measure, the 1980s are shaping up as the most entrepreneurial decade in U.S. history." [6]

Three of these measures are the dramatically changing statistics for new jobs, new businesses, and self-employment.

Creating Jobs

Small business created about 3.2 million new jobs in 1982-84 at a time large businesses created only 1.6 million new jobs, according to the U.S. Small Business Administration. Some place the percentage even higher. A Dun & Bradstreet economist expects more than half of the 2 million new workers in 1985 will be hired by firms with fewer than 100 employees.

New business incorporations set a new record at 600,400 in 1983 and are expected to top 645,000 in 1984 when the final figures are in, according to Dun & Bradstreet Corp. [7]

"The increase in self-employed workers was 13.7 percent of the total civilian employment increase between November 1982 and November 1983," the SBA stated in its 1984 report, *The State of Small Business.* [8]

We recently led a roundtable discussion on entrepreneurial spirit and risk management for some professional affiliates at the Direct Marketing Idea Exchange in New York City. The "DMIX," founded by Nat Ross nearly fifteen years ago, attracts about 100 top level New York direct marketing pros to its every-other-month luncheon.

We found that 85 percent of our roundtable group of direct marketing practitioners had formed their own companies or purchased them through an insider or leveraged buyout.

Most admitted to making the move into their own businesses after years of feeling frustrated and unsatisfied as managers or officers of larger corporations.

The consensus of the group was that the motivation for entrepreneurial involvement came from one's desire to get greater control of his (or her) own future, the hope of integrating his personal life and work to a greater degree, and the wish to put his personal style and touch on his own business activities. Rewards and growth of personal assets were also expected to come faster. Two statistics supporting this forecast were that participation in the roundtable grew by 25 percent, and entrepreneurs outnumbered corporate managers three to one. [9]

Interestingly, our roundtable group agreed that the climate for entrepreneurial startups and buyouts during the 80s was being encouraged by three major economic trends:

1. A greater willingness by business managers and investors to take personal risk than in previous decades.

2. More divestitures by large corporations of smaller divisions.

3. More available capital from traditional and non-traditional financing sources.

These three major trends—entrepreneurship, deconglomeration, and available capital—are logically parallel and related. They represent the buyers, sellers, and money that are fueling the buyout boom.

As conglomeration reverts to deconglomeration, there are new opportunities and big rewards for skilled and dedicated managers who understand and are responsive to these opportunities and entrepreneurial trends.

Will the entrepreneurial boom be able to sustain itself?

We think it will.

Corporations Seeking Suitors

Diversification has proved to be unprofitable and unmanageable.

Corporations are turning to divestitures as the route to increased productivity and sales, better management, cheaper financing, and, of course, more profits.

The surge in divestitures and spinoffs has been prompted by inflation, the ready availability of buyout funds, new management techniques, the new breed of entrepreneurial risk-takers, and a stock market that turned against conglomerates.

Dick Hug, president of Environmental Elements, led an insider buyout of the Baltimore division from Koppers in 1983. Hug said the move was prompted by the recession. Koppers per-share earnings dropped from $1.58 in 1981 to 32 cents in 1982.

"The directors instructed the senior management to shrink the size of the company and divest themselves of some businesses that were out of the mainstream of Koppers's business and raise some cash to be able to pay down borrowing," Hug said. Koppers has shed about twenty-four product lines since that time.

Jack Pruitt, chairman of Harris Graphics of Melbourne, Florida, America's largest printing equipment manufacturer, led an insider buyout of the assets of the printing equipment business from Harris Corporation in 1983.

Pruitt said, "Harris Corporation acted because it had become increasingly apparent that the company was involved in two distinct businesses that were growing apart. One, of course, was the printing equipment business, accounting for approximately one-fourth of sales and earnings. The other and larger business was the manufacturing and marketing of electronic-communications and information-processing equipment.

"From a management point of view, it was felt that the growth potential of each business could best be achieved if each were under separate and independent management." [10]

Corporations are pulling away from diversification in a search for clear-cut strategies. They have frequently found it is as costly in time and resources to manage and service a small subsidiary as a major division.

This was demonstrated at Garden Way, Inc. when three product lines, a workbench, a cider press, and a "Kitchen Carousel," absorbed enormous time and management attention before being spun off, one to an insider and two to outsiders.

Increasingly, corporate managers are planning for growth by sticking to the main mission, not trying to be all things to all customers and all shareholders.

Even corporations that are not conglomerates have discovered that smaller is friendlier, more creative, and more stimulating to group performance. They are giving individuals and teams more responsibility and receiving more productivity and innovation in return. It's the Age of the Entrepreneur — even in the corporations.

Firms with more than 100 employees dropped from 51.3 percent of all business employers in 1978 to 49 percent in 1982. The SBA said this decline "may be representative of a longer-run effort in some industries to find the most efficient operating size."

A recent University of Michigan study shows that workers in groups of 600 or less are more productive than larger groups by a factor of 50 percent. [11]

The Conglomerate Era began to wither when managers and investors alike began to see that a corporation's business problems often occurred because the corporation's affairs were controlled by unknowledgeable and inexperienced outsiders from distant corporate headquarters and board rooms.

It was found that when conglomerates were able to deliver superior management expertise as promised, the skills turned out to be the cost-cutting, attention-to-detail, and human-relations skills that have been the age-old secrets to entrepreneurial success.

Today, with the corporate emphasis on strategic fit rather than diversification, oddball divisions with recurring problems are likely candidates for divestiture.

This could be disappointing to managers who remain overconfident of permanent employment with one firm. They could come to work one day and discover they have never met their boss.

Money Chasing Money

Leveraged buyouts don't take over firms, investors do.

By definition, an LBO is a useful financing tool. In practice, the technique has gotten a bad name in the hands of a few corporate raiders, the Rupert Murdochs, Carl Icahns, and T. Boone Pickenses.

Most of the publicity about leveraged buyouts is focused on the megamergers and the billion-dollar deals put together by Wall Street investment banks on behalf of heavy stock traders.

These speculative megadeals and leveraged takeovers by outside investors have little to do with insider management buyouts.

But these speculative takeover games are worth reviewing if only for the stark contrasts they provide to our friendly, insider buyouts and for a few threads of commonality which will be instructive.

The big takeover games are money games made possible because there is a lot of money around. Bank interest rates have been deregulated and bankers are permitted to accept fees as intermediaries in large deals. Inflation and interest rates are lower. Home and business borrowing have declined. Business taxes are down. The economy has moved through a recovery phase. However, no one is sure whether a rising stock market contributes to the takeover activity or whether it is the other way around.

Joining the investment banks in the takeover games are such allied firms as business brokerages, finance companies, insurance companies, and pension funds.

The megabuyouts are engineered not in the executive suites of business managers but in the war rooms of takeover lawyers and professional arbitragers.

Buyout Funds

The investment banks were slow to get into the megabucks LBO games following the lead of a few buyout firms such as Kohlberg, Kravis, Roberts & Co. When KKR assembled a $250 million buyout equity fund in 1982, *Institutional Investor* magazine called that sum "mammoth." But only two years later, KKR began assembling a new fund, this time for $1 billion.

The equity funds, as opposed to senior or subordinated debt, are "the easiest funds to raise for buyouts because of the widespread conviction among investors that they provide a way to get rich," according to *Institutional Investor*. [12]

The LBO craze has been fueled by the glamour surrounding some spectacular buyouts of large public corporations. Notable is the reported $82 million that former Treasury Secretary William E. Simon made on his $330,000 investment in his 1983 buyout of Gibson Greeting Cards. [13]

Wall Street observers said in early 1984 that the only firms still safe from leveraged buyout attacks were General Motors and IBM. Later, some observers said GM looked vulnerable.

Overpricing Feared

All of this causes some LBO professionals to worry about overpriced deals resulting from too much money chasing too few deals. It's no wonder: few investments offer greater returns than those found in many strategic corporate takeovers.

The investment firms are on the trail of annual returns as high as 40 to 60 percent of capital invested. These are the returns reportedly earned by Kohlberg, Kravis, Roberts & Co. the nation's leading LBO house.

Buying all of a public firm's outstanding shares and taking it private give investors a chance to restructure the firm's accounting system in private without having to report to shareholders or the Securities and Exchange Commission.

"Credit much of the success of LBOs to our terrible tax laws, especially to the indefensible corporate income tax," financial writer Allan Sloan said in *Forbes* magazine. [14]

Strategy

Debt can be reduced by selling off assets, including subsidiaries, under the theory that the parts are frequently worth more than the whole.

Then, within a few years, the buyout investors can go public again with an offering that is more saleable while they benefit from low capital gains tax rates on their stock sales.

All of this juggling of financial resources is primarily for the benefit of investors and lenders who are interested in an immediate high rate of return rather than a steady growth in income and employment over a decade.

It assumes the increased debt load will not prove too burdensome for management. Management's view of the juggling usually depends on how badly they need their jobs or whether they were invited to share in the ownership.

In most LBOs initiated by outsiders, managers are lucky to know what's going on and very lucky if invited to buy stock in what amounts to a shotgun wedding.

Corporate raiders frequently announce their plans for a buyout of a target firm with a promise to increase shareholder earnings by trimming the fat from the operations. Managers who are not trimmed with the fat will be kept lean and mean managing the corporation's new leveraged debt load.

Two Views of the LBO

Predictably, the LBO boom has led to two schools of thought.

The advocates say LBOs are healthy for shareholders as a way to revive a sleepy firm with new owners who will build values and reduce the acquisition debt once the old owners and incompetent managers are out of the way.

The best way to avoid a hostile takeover, according to takeover advocate and practitioner Sir James Goldsmith, chairman of General Oriental Investments, Ltd., "...is to manage successfully and, thereby, to earn a sturdy stock market rating." [15]

The critics say many of the leveraged takeovers are greed-oriented deals shaped by predatory, outside money managers and arbitragers who are gambling on the cooperation of management and employees to pay off their new debt and build capital values once the old owners are out of the way.

Speaking for the critics, management professor Peter F. Drucker said, "It is increasingly hard to defend the unfriendly takeover as benefiting anyone other than the raider [and a few investment bankers and merger lawyers]." [16]

Another critic, investment banker Felix G. Rohatyn, known as "Mr. Fixit" for saving New York City from bankruptcy, warned of the "buyout binge" in a May, 1984, speech to newspaper editors, saying, "We are turning the financial markets into a huge casino."

Rohatyn said a typical takeover turns a public company with $100 million in debt and $900 million in equity into a private company with $900 million in debt and $100 million in equity.

Rohatyn said the deals drafted by his fellow investment bankers and other LBO professionals were betting on two factors, continued growth and lower interest rates, with no margin for error.

Debt burden can become unsupportable if interest rates rise or if the stock market takes a nosedive and drags down the value of securities placed with lenders as collateral.

John S. R. Shad, chairman of the Securities and Exchange Commission, said the leveraging of corporate America had changed Darwin's survival of the fittest into "acquire or be acquired."

Shad said, "The threat of being taken over is an inducement to curtail research and development, plant rehabilitation and expansion, and other programs entailing current costs for long-term benefits." [17]

And so vulnerable corporations have become distracted from their main mission and their attention to customers while they focus on maximum returns, quarterly earnings growth, and "equity kickers" for speculators.

Investment banks were the major force behind the conglomeration boom of the 1960s and they have been a major force in the leveraged buyout boom of the 1980s.

Moves For Managers

Understanding this, alert business managers who want to keep control of their business and personal lives will find low-profile ways to work around the edges of the speculative, leveraged buyout trend.

Tom Begel, president of Pullman Transportation, took his company out of The Signal Companies as a spinout rather than a leveraged buyout. Pullman is still a public company and Begel and his employees continue to invest in Pullman — and themselves — by purchasing stock in the public markets.

"I think a lot of leveraged buyouts are being done for no particular reason other than someone smells an opportunity to make some money. A lot of money gets loaned and debt gets accumulated, and I'm not sure it's in everybody's best interests," Begel said.

The lesson in all of this for professional managers is that in the big money game, it is the player with the big money who writes the rules and wins the game.

The LBO And The IBO

This, of course, is not true with the insider buyout. And this is but one of the many profound differences between the two. Here are some others:

In an LBO, the emphasis is on the investors, leveraging their money with the power of the corporation's assets. In an IBO, the emphasis is on a manager or several managers, leveraging their skills, knowledge, and position with the power of loans and the corporation's assets.

A typical LBO is primarily an investment and financing device. A typical IBO is a management and financing device.

In an LBO controlled by outsiders, the managers often are the losers because they are not managing change. Change is managing them, and the managers will be lucky if they manage to hold onto their jobs.

Thus, an LBO, most likely, is something that happens to a manager. An IBO is something that a manager makes happen.

In an IBO, the manager is managing the deal. For an aggressive, far-sighted manager, the IBO, the insider's deal, may be the best defense against an LBO, the outsider's deal.

LBOs result from a particular set of economic conditions. These conditions must exist or there will be no reason to attempt an LBO.

Not so the IBO. As you read this book, you will realize the IBO is a tool that can be used in good times and bad, whenever there is a need for a corporation to restructure itself in some way. The alert manager will be prepared to take advantage of this opportunity.

Profile of a Target

"There is still plenty of venture capital around, financial people looking to make a buck. There are still plenty of opportunities with mismatched companies and products," according to Larry Munini, president of Genesys Software Systems.

"The bad news is that, like all good things, leveraged buyouts are showing signs of wretched excess," Allan Sloan said in *Forbes* in April, 1984. [14]

"The increasing popularity of leveraged buyouts has attracted inexperienced players resulting in poorly planned deals," Tomislava Simic, Grimm's research director, said.

You'll be lucky to do one successful insider buyout in your lifetime. Do one deal and you'll be a veteran.

For how-to-do-it advice on insider buyouts, we turn to IBO veterans such as those who have contributed to this book.

However, there is also a lot we can learn from a group of veteran buyers, some of whom have participated in dozens or hundreds of deals, namely, outside investors and intermediaries.

If you are considering an insider buyout, it will be worth your time to take a step back and look at your division from the perspective of a veteran buyout manager or investor to see whether it meets certain tests.

Small, Friendly Deals

All deals considered, most outsider buyouts are small and reasonably friendly deals. It is only the large, unfriendly ones that capture the headlines and give a bad name to the business.

The outside investors are looking for features that make a corporation sound, but they are also looking for specific features that are essential in making a leveraged buyout possible.

These are the same features that will be important to you in assessing whether your division qualifies for an insider buyout.

Most important in a leveraged buyout is a substantial cash flow. That means enough cash to cover operations and then some. It means dependable, predictable income that will convince lenders their participation is safe and the debt will be discharged on time.

A target firm must also have substantial assets. Some assets such as real estate, subsidiaries, and inventory are especially desirable because they can be sold to cover the acquisition debt.

Other assets such as buildings and equipment are valuable to buyers who will take maximum advantage of depreciation allowances to shelter income.

Over-funded pension plans are as good as cash to new owners who can buy a cheaper plan and use the surplus to retire debt.

A target firm is also likely to show good growth potential in an industry with many competitors, no one of which is dominant.

The target firm's near-term capital requirements should be minimal, and the company should not be facing an expensive retooling or technological breakthrough in its industry.

In the case of a public firm, the stock should be undervalued, that is, trading on the stock market at a level which does not reflect the true value of its assets, earnings, or cash flow.

Similarly, in the case of a private firm, the selling price should be a bargain with the sellers seeking benefits in something other than fair market value.

Typically, a target firm will also have good leveragability with little debt — less than 40 percent of equity.

In other words, a likely LBO target is a good, sound, mature business. Not very dynamic, perhaps, but a safe investment with some slack that can be mined by aggressive investors, or, in the case of an insider buyout, manager-owners.

And, oh yes, according to professional buyout managers, a worthy target will also be characterized by another feature: capable management.

Moves of New Owners

However, in the case of an outsider buyout, the new owners may want to cut the fat. This means eliminating pet projects, valuable properties, and, for sure, some long-time employees. They may even want to liquidate the corporation or move it out of town. They may ask for your opinion. Then again, they may not.

Other Options For Insiders

The manager of a division that has all the characteristics of a typical takeover or spinoff prospect has four choices: turn it around, resign, ride it out, or buy it out.

If a takeover, spinoff, or sellout begins to materialize, he may have two additional choices: buy in or fight it out.

Once the deal has been cast, he may have lost his options to buy in or even to remain employed by the firm.

To obtain maximum control of your business and personal life, we recommend an insider buyout: a friendly management buyout of a subsidiary or division which puts ownership into the hands of the top manager or the top few managers — into your hands.

However, there are other options you could face with large groups of co-workers and outside investors, such as a management buyout or an employee buyout. These are deals that would keep ownership and control out of your hands and perhaps out of the company.

The Management Buyout

A management buyout, as the term is commonly used, means new outside owners have purchased a company in a deal that is partially financed by a stake from management.

Such a management buyout typically begins when management seeks to counter a takeover or sellout threat with a buyout offer of its own. A few top managers begin by seeking equity commitments from among themselves. But some managers are not ready to buy in. Time is short. The insider investor group becomes hard to manage at hastily called, secret informational meetings. There are hard feelings about family stress, unequal participation, and the need to rewrite home mortgages.

The next step usually is to retain an investment banker or venture capitalist to help assemble the deal and round up some other investors.

Typically, the investment banker will require a 10 to 25 percent equity commitment from management — enough to hold their feet to the fire but not enough so they can seize control.

Also, the lenders will typically demand an equity position, possibly a majority position.

What begins as a management buyout may eventually become a mere management-initiated buyout with management holding only a minority position and facing the risk of a short honeymoon with new partners.

Employee Buyout

Employee buyouts are vastly different from manager buyouts in that the buyers as a group are all clustered at the bottom of the company hierarchy.

Bona fide employee buyouts of major firms happen very infrequently — for example, only about sixty times in the 1972-82 decade. During that period, all but two of the buyouts succeeded.

But there are enough so that there is a national association for them.

We are watching the possible development of one right now in our neighboring town of North Adams, where employees of the Sprague Electric Co. Brown Street plant are preparing a buyout offer for the parent company, Penn Central Co., to avoid an eventual closing of the capacitor manufacturing plant.

An employee buyout is often the last resort before liquidation. The parent company has closed the plant and made plans to move the equipment out of town. The employees have skills not usable elsewhere in the community.

The employees as a group become pitted in negotiations against groups of unfamiliar officials from corporate headquarters. For the situation to have developed this far, there is likely to be little love lost between the parties.

Negotiations are eventually conducted in the full glare of public concern about possible loss of jobs. The talks may even attract the participation of the governor of the state and network television cameras. The workers have few cards to play except the threat to create a local public relations embarrassment for the parent company.

The financing of employee buyouts may be unwieldy and risky. But there is one compelling reason for finding public money: the alternative is closing the plant and losing the payroll.

Even with guaranteed financing, there's much that can go wrong with an employee buyout. One example is resistance by labor union leaders to wage cuts while they continue to fight old wars with officials from the departing parent company.

At best, ownership and control in an employee buyout are likely to be diluted among the employees and complicated by local politics. Management finds itself stripped of staff services formerly provided by headquarters, including a line of credit. And the quasi-public nature of the buyout could prove inhibiting to customers, lenders, and talented new management recruits.

Participating in an employee buyout or a management buyout with dozens of managers and outsiders holding a majority position is not the way to get control of your business life or participate in the entrepreneurial revival.

Your Role

If your whole company or division is not available, perhaps you can focus on a few key assets which will give you a start on nurturing your own business.

But to obtain maximum control over your own life, you will need to show your intentions before someone else puts a different plan into action.

If a group of your superiors or associates begins plans for a large-group management or employee buyout, it probably is too late for you to try to walk away with a key division.

Participating in a large-group buyout may be precisely the compromise you seek between remaining with the corporation and seeking employment elsewhere.

On the other hand, if your entrepreneurial instincts have you dreaming of being the boss in your own shop, a group partnership may be even less satisfactory than your arm's length relationship with a corporate employer.

Now Is The Time

The buyout of a corporation or one of its divisions sounds like a perfectly reasonable business investment — unless you are the manager of the target business and you learned of the deal in the morning newspaper.

In that case, the acquisition probably sounds to you like a takeover or a sellout.

Someone could be auditing your employer's corporation at this very moment, studying its potential as a buyout or takeover target.

Your best defense is a good offense. The time is right for managers of non-fit subsidiaries to make plans for solving their business problems, creating personal wealth, and taking control of their lives all in one deal — with an insider buyout.

Merrill Halpern, the president of Charterhouse Group International, Inc., a venture capital firm that takes a controlling interest in acquired companies, spoke at a 1984 roundtable sponsored by *Mergers & Acquisitions* magazine about the deconglomeration and buyout trend. [18]

"I'm convinced that the thrust of the large deals in the future will be megadeals broken up into small companies," Halpern said. "You'll see a lot of second-level LBOs following first-level LBOs."

Opportunities

This sounds like fertile territory for insider buyouts for these are the kind of deals that escape the bidding wars of the takeover artists. The kind of deals that rarely attract much public attention, especially when they are merely an asset buyout. The kind of deals that are first discussed by the parties over coffee in the company cafeteria, not by unknown investors in an attorney's office in New York.

How would you be affected by a wave of spinoffs, divestitures, and buyouts?

The time is right for both inside and outside investors who want to take an equity position in the buyouts.

Wall Street observers see a cooling in the rush to take over large public corporations partially because the economy has cooled, partially because the most vulnerable prospects have been acquired, and partially because of increasing caution by lenders in the wake of the collapse of Continental Illinois National Bank & Trust Co. of Chicago. This should help make capital available for more private company buyouts, especially friendly, win-win management buy-outs.

Finances Look Good

You may find grassroots business sellers and lenders more and more reluctant to endorse a high-risk business plan if the emphasis is on managing a leveraged buyout as opposed to managing a business. But you will have no trouble finding financing for a friendly, win-win buyout of a going business by experienced, trusted management.

The time is also right for corporations that want to sell oddball divisions that are causing management problems.

What makes an underachieving, oddball division become successful simply because it is pulled out of a large corporation and made to stand on its own?

Tom Begel of Pullman Transportation tells us: "The two companies we acquired are now suddenly part of a much smaller company, and they're running a hell of a lot more efficiently than they ever ran as part of a big corporation.

"And the simple reason for that is we are giving them a whole lot more time and attention because they are a very vital interest to us where they were only of marginal interest in a multi-billion dollar environment.

"For the individual business itself, it has been a very healthy thing. And for the people working for these companies, it has been a very healthy thing.

"Creating more jobs as we grow, we're tending to pay people a little better because they are very important to us — they are not part of a multi-billion dollar corporation.

"I expect managers and staff and second- and third-line managers in this company are making more money now than they ever made in the larger corporate environment."

Take Control

The time is also right for managers and employees who want to take more control of their personal and business lives.

In many takeovers and buyouts, corporate employees, including managers without equity, have been treated like commodities, like the equipment and the inventory. Managers and employees are increasingly learning how to fight takeover plans in the political and public relations arenas.

And the new employee stock option plan (ESOP) provisions adopted by Congress in 1984 give managers and employees valuable new tools to ward off takeover or sellout plans that would be harmful to local interests.

Ray Gould, president of Memorex, which was acquired in December 1981 by Burroughs, said the merger and acquisition activity today is of an entirely different character from that of the 1960s and 1970s.

"In the [merger] relationship [today], both companies are reaching out for something the other has. This was not the case in the era of the conglomerates, and so perhaps we have gone from the era of the conglomerate to the era of the strategic relationship," Gould told *Inc.* magazine. [19]

Today's best deals are not built on any old company and any old owner. They are founded on a strategic relationship between a particular firm and a particular buyer.

If you have a strategic relationship with your division, go for it. Why should you be divorced from your job, your company, your friends, and perhaps your community because of the speculative decisions of outside, distant money managers?

You are a money manager. And an investor. What's more, speaking of strategic positioning, you are also an inside manager.

We cannot tell you for sure which comes first in an insider buyout — the entrepreneur or the opportunity. Whichever, it is clear that buyouts, entrepreneurs, and new business are all on a growth curve.

Your Position Today

You have read this chapter and now understand the trends in corporations nationwide. Before going on to the next chapter, take a minute to think how these trends could affect you. Answer these questions to start yourself thinking.

In this age of deconglomeration, are you the manager of an oddball division, an underachiever, a sleepy program that has long been ignored and ill-appreciated? If yes, do you realize that you're head, too, of a major company problem?

How long will your company tolerate the losses your division is ringing up?

Would it welcome a buyout, a sale of assets, any move that would rid it of this problem division?

Are corporation officials ready to spend what it would take to energize your division? Or would they prefer the easy way — get rid of it?

Who else understands the value of your division and its potential? Who else understands the value of your efforts?

How secure are you in your position?

How much time do you have before the company will act?

Recognize this danger. The sword may be hanging. Recognize that it is imperative for you to act before the company makes a decisive move of its own.

You have always believed in your product and its potential in the right environment. You have believed in your abilities as a businessman and a manager.

It is time to assess your standing, to decide whether your situation fits for an IBO.

If you feel your corporation is preparing to make some move regarding your division, simply waiting to see what happens may mean that you've lost a golden opportunity to achieve independence to run a business of your own, the way it should be run.

You may think you and the company are at odds and miles apart on the future of your division. The truth is, you may be thinking very much along the same track. You agree that there's no place in the corporation or its future plans for your division. You agree that it's a time to make a decision, and that could be to chop off the division or to take some equally drastic step. You agree that, no matter what, the division needs some new thinking, new ideas, new approaches.

And you're ready, as they would expect you to be, to make some of those changes that seem so essential to both of you.

Chapter II References:

[1] *Does Technology Really Create Jobs?* by Tom Richman, quoting Massachusetts Institute of Technology researcher David Birch; *Inc.*, August 1984.

[2] *Managers in the Conglomerate Era*, by Stanley C. Vance, Wiley-Interscience, 1971.

[3] Grimm's figures include no deals worth less than $500,000 and few under $5 million. There are no reliable buyout statistics available for small, private, closely held firms, a group that constitutes the vast majority of companies.

[4] *The Wall Street Journal*, December 22, 1983, page 1; *U.S. News & World Report*, February 6, 1984, page 84.

[5] Statistical Report on Mergers and Acquisitions, Federal Trade Commission, 1979.

[6] "There's No Stopping Now," by Kevin Farrell, *Venture*, February 1985.

[7] "Business Incorporations Climb," Dun & Bradstreet Corp., re: Associated Press, February 17, 1985.

[8] *The State of Small Business: A Report of the President*, U.S. Small Business Administration, March 1984.

[9] "Entrepreneurial Spirit and Risk Management," moderated by M. John Storey and Donald Dubendorf, Direct Marketing Idea Exchange, New York City, November 14, 1984.

[10] "Harris Graphics...The Inside Story," an interview with Jack Pruitt, chairman of Harris Graphics, *The PIA Communicator*, Printing Industries of America, Inc., July/August 1983.

[11] Hay Group, University of Michigan and Strategic Planning Institute, *The Wall Street Journal*, July 3, 1984.

[12] "Wall Street finally discovers the leveraged buyout," by Linda Sandlers, *Institutional Investor*, August 1982.

[13] *The Wall Street Journal,* July 25, 1984; *Venture,* March 1984.

[14] "Luring Banks Overboard," by Allan Sloan, *Forbes,* April 9, 1984.

[15] "Hostile Takeovers Easier to Swallow Than Poison Pills," by James Goldsmith, *The Wall Street Journal,* February 11, 1985.

[16] "Taming the Corporate Takeover," by Peter F. Drucker, *The Wall Street Journal,* October 30, 1984.

[17] "The Leveraging of America," by John S. R. Shad, in a speech to the New York Financial Writers Association, July 1984.

[18] "Roundtable, The Leveraged Buyout Market," by Eleanor Allen, *Mergers & Acquisitions,* Summer 1984.

[19] "Let a Thousand Flowers Bloom," by Eugene Linden, *Inc.,* April 1984.

Chapter III

The Alternatives

You've seen it coming and you called it exactly right. The corporation has decided to do something about your division. What to do hasn't been decided. As head of the division, you're asked to explore the alternatives, report on them, and make your recommendations. At least there's a comfortable feel to the decision to go to you first for recommendations.

You recognize your responsibility is to the corporation, that you must recommend a course of action that reflects the long-run best interests of the corporation.

Manager's Best-Case Scenario

We suggest that you prepare for making those recommendations by completing a study for your use alone. Let's call this the Manager's Best-Case Scenario.

This is not a buyout plan or a business plan or a plan for reaching your personal goals for life.

This is the trusted manager's plan for energizing his division under ideal circumstances. What is missing and needed? What is unnecessary and should be eliminated?

The Manager's Best-Case Scenario is an informal, unofficial report to yourself, the manager. This is not a self-serving project but a decision-making, brainstorming technique.

The Manager's Best-Case Scenario is the vision of what the

division could be from the unique and dispassionate perspective of the trusted corporate official, the division's chief-operations officer — you.

Doing a Manager's Best-Case Scenario is an exercise in looking beyond your current problems with personnel, communications, and finance to an ideal production and marketing cycle.

The scenario should be a supplement to your planning process regardless of your personal, long-term plans with the company. This is not a plan that relates to you personally but a plan that relates to your job.

Write this scenario in company terms, on company time, without any prejudice towards personalities or personnel problems. Write it so that it can take its place with your other planning documents and be shared with company officials later if the occasion arises.

Preparing the best-case scenario will force you to rephrase your dissatisfaction with your division's performance in positive terms from a corporate point of view.

When you are finished, the resulting best-case goals may seem unrealistic or unattainable in the light of existing circumstances. This is to be expected. One purpose of this exercise is to prepare you for studying how to close the gap between an ideal division's best-case goals and the current circumstances.

As a senior level manager, you are expected to produce short- or long-term management plans for your division. You are probably a part of the company's ongoing strategic planning and spend time in planning exercises each month. You have in your files management plans with components for such things as cash flow, sales, production, personnel, marketing, contingencies, and long-range growth strategies.

So it should be no problem now for you to do the planning necessary to review quickly best-case scenarios before deciding upon the best alternatives for your division.

Prepare your best-case scenario with a vision of ideal but nameless and faceless managers and employees in mind.

Remember, this is not the manager's management plan. This is the manager's wish list — a list of goals from the manager's unique perspective.

If you had it all to do over again and you were the final authority, what would you put in the budget and what would you leave out?

Regardless of the description in the corporation's annual report, what industry is your division really in? What is your division's specific business? Who is your real competition? What is your optimum market share?

A Clarifying Experience

At Garden Way, Inc., there was a perfect opportunity to do this when top management, with the help of an outside consulting firm, entered into its first strategic planning exercise.

This was developed with care internally, and each key manager was asked to put his thoughts down on paper regarding the future of his division.

I did this for Garden Way Publishing and Garden Way Research (a division of the company that manufactured several products, including garden carts), and found the exercise a very helpful, clarifying experience. Different from budgets and cash flow planning, the first strategic planning statement was a real, longer-term effort at thinking and planning.

Major Sections

Your Manager's Best-Case Scenario should consist of at least three major sections:

1. The goals for the division from the perspective of the manager's office. What are the division's most promising opportunities in the order of their importance? What is a realistic deadline for seizing each of these opportunities under ideal circumstances?

Where are your most profitable markets? What is your biggest sustainable competitive advantage? What would be the ideal mix of personnel and facilities to meet that market's demands and opportunities?

What could be done to improve productivity? What are your division's most pressing unmet needs? What are the most serious threats facing your division? How could they be resolved?

2. A clear statement of the strategy necessary to reach the goals. What products or services could be offered? By what production and delivery process? How soon? For how long? From which locations? To which customers? At what expenditure of resources?

3. A summary of the resources headquarters must provide the division if the goals are to be reached.

Add to this the additional authority that needs to be vested with the division to achieve the best-case scenario.

Finally add the responsibilities and distractions that headquarters must remove from the division under the best-case circumstances.

Only after all three of these managerial perspectives are completed will it be time to compare and choose among alternatives for the corporation.

Now ask yourself these questions: How does your best-case scenario differ from the plans you have prepared according to corporate guidelines? Will headquarters ever meet the best-case managerial needs? Has it ever tried?

What remedies by headquarters are possible? What steps by headquarters are probable?

If you do it well, this report will assist you as you move forward toward studying the alternatives and deciding which is best for the corporation.

Studying the Alternatives

You have several alternatives — a turnaround, selling the business, liquidating it. Let's look at these the way you must, as a trusted corporation executive whose goal is to recommend what's best for the corporation. Study these alternatives, look particularly at the negative side of each one, and try to add other negative and positive points that fit your particular case.

Managing a Turnaround

Turning around a troubled division or subsidiary heads the wish list of every loyal corporation employee.

If, in the past, you haven't been able to do the job alone, headquarters could decide now to give you some help and crank up your division with new resources and revitalized commitments.

Although a turnaround is clearly the favorite alternative, it may not always be possible or even desirable. Not all doggy divisions are salvageable.

To be salvageable, a troubled company or division needs strengths to build upon: a good cash flow, a strong customer base, and suitably situated plants with adequate equipment. A turnaround prospect also needs alert, capable, and willing management with strong support from headquarters.

If your division has all the essentials, and headquarters promises to spend the time and money needed to energize your division, you may be in luck.

If, on the other hand, headquarters announces it will focus its turnaround try on the parent corporation's problems, your worst fears of an uncertain future for your troubled division may be coming true, and you may be in trouble.

If the turnaround is merely a squeeze play — an order from headquarters for your division to cut expenses while boosting sales — you are most certainly in trouble.

If the "new resources" for your division means bringing in a turnaround specialist who will prepare personnel reviews on division employees, including you, you also may be in trouble. This would be a sign headquarters believes the division problems lie more within your division than from any lack of headquarters support. You can only hope that you get along very well with the turnaround specialist and are able to make him or her your advocate at headquarters.

From the corporate standpoint, there are definite negative aspects to a turnaround. Address these.

1. Burden on the corporation. It will take money, time, and talent away from other corporate activities, activities that might prove to be better money-earners for the corporation.

2. May fail. The attempted turnaround will lead to a period of uncertainty, with no guarantee of success in the end.

3. May be costly. There is the definite possibility that an attempted turnaround will be throwing good money after bad.

Before endorsing a turnaround, ask yourself, what is different now that will make the turnaround succeed?

Is this a serious commitment designed to overcome known problems, or is this merely a public relations effort to smooth over problems?

If a turnaround could be successful, what has prevented it before this, and how has this situation been corrected?

If you could manage a turnaround, why haven't you?

Do you think you can solve the problems of your division or subsidiary within the existing corporate framework?

Seeking a Suitor

If your divisional problems persist, you need to be prepared for the moment during an executive committee meeting when someone says of your division, "Let's shop it. Find out what it's worth."

This is not an unusual conclusion. In addition to the divestitures we discussed in the previous chapter, companies are bought and merged at the rate of about fifty a week in this country.

Potential buyers include U.S. companies looking to expand or diversify and foreign buyers seeking a U.S. base of operations. And confirming the trend toward smaller companies, dealmakers report there are more prospective company buyers among individuals or small groups of investors today than there are companies for sale.

How marketable is your division? Are any third parties desperately in pursuit of it? Would your division fit easily within another company?

Maybe there is nothing wrong with your division that a strategic relationship with a new owner couldn't solve.

The sale of your no-fit division to a more suitable corporation could be a bonanza for the division as well as the buyer and the seller if it results in new life for the division and relief from problems for your parent corporation. This would be a win-win-win transaction.

On the other hand, it would not be hard to imagine a transaction that would result in a lose-lose-lose scenario.

As the division manager, you must consider a multitude of things before recommending that your division be put on the block. What happens to you personally is not one of them.

Your fiduciary responsibilities to your employer require that you assist in the wise management of the corporation's assets even if this means selling off your workplace. You could be offered a transfer within your company. Or you could be offered a career by the buyer. Or you could find your services are no longer needed by either firm.

Again, there are negative aspects to a sale to be considered. Study them before making your recommendations.

1. It's inconvenient. Outsiders will be in your offices for a thorough review of your company and division records. The prospective buyers and their agents may expect you to provide them with office space and secretarial help in poring through your books, sales records, trade secrets, and errors. This can be a prolonged and exasperating experience.

2. It can lead to leaks. Confidential information gained by outsiders during such shopping trips frequently winds up in the files of competitors or regulators if the deal falls through.

3. It takes time. The negotiations for a sale will probably string out over a lengthy period. Meanwhile, the outside suitors take the time to learn your business, using delays to their advantage while your production time is wasted, sales momentum is stalled, operating decisions are postponed, and perhaps some of your key people leave in frustration.

4. It can be unpleasant. The process is not built on trust. Both parties have much to fear in acting on insufficient information and losing control of the transaction. But all odds, the parties will be entering into a competitive encounter with little hope of establishing a long-term, cooperative relationship.

5. There's no chance for "win-win." The sales of subsidiaries are not noted for evolving into win-win deals. Most likely the party with the bigger problem entering the negotiations will wind up as the comparative loser.

The sellers must ask themselves, "How much do we want to give up to rid ourselves of this problem?"

6. There are no guarantees. A deal that collapses after a lengthy, expensive courtship will leave hard feelings on both sides. It could be a lose-lose effort.

7. Your image can tarnish. Your standing in the business world may suffer. When your competitors find out about the proposed sale, they'll tell news reporters and your customers, "I hear their business is on the block."

Liquidation

Of all the alternatives for a corporation trying to solve problems with a misfit division or subsidiary, liquidation is the one least likely to be used and the one most associated with a failing company.

Liquidation sounds so negative, so terminal. People tend to think liquidation is code for failure, bankruptcy, or worse. The term is generally associated with forced liquidation in bankruptcy proceedings, and thus its bad name. But what we are talking about here is voluntary liquidation.

If your superiors and associates are thinking about liquidating your division, they will probably first talk about it behind your back. You need to be alert to the signals that something is going on.

Depending on individual circumstances, a division or subsidiary may be worth more when sold in pieces than if it is sold as a going business. Similarly, it may be easier to dissolve a division and sell it in pieces than it is to sell it as a going business. What's more, dissolving a subsidiary and selling it in pieces does not necessarily mean the business ends, if the pieces are large enough.

For example, Valle's Steak House, a family-managed chain of thirty New England restaurants and other properties, was put on the block in 1979, shortly after the death of the founder. Members of the family, including the founder's widow, owned 67 percent of the public corporation. When no buyer was found after two years, the corporation was taken private in 1982 in an insider buyout by management and members of the founding family. The new officers since then have methodically liquidated the properties on an individual basis. [1]

Liquidation as a problem-solving alternative thus depends upon liquidity — the immediate value of your division's assets on the open market.

Liquidation is an especially attractive alternative for a corporation that wants to get fair market value for properties that have been heavily depreciated and reflect little value on the balance sheet.

If a corporation publicized in advance its intent to liquidate a division's assets, the resulting furor among employees could cripple sales. Therefore, firms going into liquidation will frequently move quickly and secretly. This kind of a piecemeal but simultaneous sale of a division's assets is usually conducted in a series of hush-hush transactions with only the highest corporate officers involved. Employees and some suppliers may suspect something's happening, but they are generally distracted by diversionary tactics and disclaimers.

Although liquidation seems to mean "killing" the business by dismemberment, this need not be the case. It could simply mean separating the assets into two or more groups, those that are needed to keep the business going under a new owner, and those that are not necessary to the business — a plant in a high-rent area, for example — and can be sold separately at a much higher price.

In fact, the parent company could liquidate your division in a series of transactions, one of which could result in an insider buyout for you if you are alert and prepared.

For example, your division's record of earnings may make it worth little as a going business to an outsider, but the assets may be of considerable value at fair market prices to firms in related businesses.

In this case, you may be able to acquire the assets you need to put yourself in business while your corporation markets the leftovers.

It was through the process of exploring various alternatives for Applied Magnetics of Santa Barbara that the idea was born for selling the Key Electro Sonic (now Key Technology) division in

Oregon to Tom Madsen's management group. The parent corporation had been considering various ways, including self-liquidation,
to raise capital.

The result was that Applied Magnetic's chairman, Harold Frank,
and another private investor helped Madsen and three other managers raise the equity for their insider buyout of Key.

In most leveraged buyouts, the new owner immediately sells off
unneeded assets to reduce debt and concentrate on the main business of the buy-out. Rupert Murdoch did this in his recent acquisition of seven TV stations from Metromedia for $2 billion. Part of
the deal is to sell off TV station WCVB in Boston to Frank Bennack
of Hearst, raising $450 million. Ted Turner's entire strategy for
taking over CBS also depended on a post-buyout assets sale.

In a liquidation, the parent corporation sells the pieces and
collects the cash for its own account. In many cases, a combination
buyout-liquidation works to the advantage of the person conducting the insider buyout, as liquidation effectively lowers the purchase
price and permits immediate and undistracted attention to the
business purchased.

Once more, and briefly, the possible negative aspects of liquidation:

1. Money is lost. Assets generally are sold at less than true value.

2. The effect on your corporation. The business world — your
suppliers, customers, all those with whom you do business — will
see it as a drastic move.

3. PR problems. Liquidation can mean a public relations nightmare, with layoffs, plant closings, unemployment, and hard feelings.

Despite these bad possibilities, liquidation is a practical and
valuable alternative for a corporation that is trying to solve problems with a misfit division.

You will want to give this alternative a fair and thorough review
in your search for what's best for the corporation. Then you will be
prepared if someone at a board meeting suggests that you kindly
consider the benefits to the corporation of cashing out your
division.

If you have been wrestling with latent, entrepreneurial insider buyout instincts, may you be so lucky.

Assessing Your Options

It's time to step to one side and consider the impact of the various alternatives for the corporation on your career, your family, and your nest egg.

You are a trusted member of the corporate family. You have financial responsibilities to the firm and its owners or shareholders. You are a key player in corporate decision-making. You will be called upon to assist in the evaluation of alternatives. It's important to you that your integrity not be compromised at any point in this process.

Nonetheless, you also have responsibilities to yourself and your family. The problems with your division will force you to clarify your personal and professional goals. You must be ready to seize your own opportunities.

Some of the alternatives cited above provide protections and liquidity for shareholders, corporate officers, and, to a lesser extent, other members of top management.

However, some of the variations provide few or no safeguards for management and employees. And some of the alternatives consist mostly of hazards.

An attempted division turnaround that failed could find you at home sending out resumes and reading the classified ads. So could a partial liquidation.

It's time to pause to measure your commitment to the firm — and its commitment to you.

You are a top level business manager earning a comfortable salary with an annual bonus and generous perquisites. You probably have some equity as a shareholder.

You are confident of your management ability and have always believed the corporation needed you more than you needed it. You have always felt optimistic about your chances for success and your ability to make things work better within the firm.

You have been taught that it didn't matter what division you headed, that your skills were transferable from job to job.

But business managers, unlike corporations, have complicated personal preferences and relationships which will vastly alter the range of career alternatives from individual to individual.

What It Takes

It takes brains, technical skills, and a certain amount of courage to find lifelong success in a competitive corporation. A career manager must also have the right personality, project the right image, and excel in human relations. And to be successful, a career manager also needs the intense desire to play a leading role in the corporate culture and enjoy the salary, the power, the people, perks, and prestige.

Many managers plan to remain with their employers and keep moving up the corporate pyramid until retirement.

If you are such a manager and your division is in trouble, these are indeed unfortunate circumstances which will require hard thinking and tough decisions. For there is a risk that your current problems with a misfit division will permanently scar your reputation in the firm.

In his 1984 book, *Managing*, former ITT Chairman Harold Geneen writes of the impact mistakes or even perceived mistakes could have on a manager's career:

"In sizable corporations, an executive on his way up has to make at least five brilliant moves before he is considered on the fast track; one mistake will plant a seed of distrust that may destroy his career." [2]

You may be able to avoid such errors if you concentrate now on assessing your strengths and weaknesses and your standing with your corporation under varied circumstances:

• Your security in your current position.
• Your backing by corporate leaders.
• The possibility of revitalization of your division.
• The possible success of such a turnaround.

- Your role in a turnaround.
- Your status if the division were sold.
- Your status if the division were liquidated.
- Your status if nothing happens.

Considered Alternatives

Most of the contributors to this book agonized through the long process of considering alternatives for their employers, their divisions, and themselves before making the move to buy their own business.

At The Signal Companies in 1982, Tom Begel, now president of the Pullman Transportation Co., said, "My range of options narrowed down to either staying with the corporation or spinning this company out. They wanted to spin it out so that question came down to their decision and my decision to go with it.

"I viewed it as the right opportunity at the right point of life," Begel said.

When Dick Hug, president of Environmental Elements, was asked by Koppers to sell the subsidiary, Hug said, "I was envisioning selling it to XYZ Company and then going to work for them as president of the operation or subsidiary or however it was structured.

"I had been a corporate professional manager all my life, for twenty-six years [ten years as president of Environmental Elements]. That's where my expertise was and that's where my experience was.

"But the more I got involved in it, the more I realized, hey, maybe this is something I can do on my own."

Hug and a group of top managers did get involved and wound up owning 74 percent of Environmental Elements which they bought from Koppers in 1983.

When Applied Magnetics put Key Electro Sonic on the block in 1982, prospective buyers were ushered around the plant at Milton-Freewater, Oregon, by the division president, Tom Madsen.

"Most of the people who were looking at buying Key were also looking at keeping the management," Madsen said. "The management here was relatively young, yet we had quite a few years' experience with Key."

If that didn't work out, Madsen said he probably would have sought a management position with another food industry company.

But Madsen and three other top managers decided that job security was not worth passing up the opportunity of a lifetime. The partners pooled their resources, secured the financing, and successfully completed an insider buyout of the food-processing equipment business.

Madsen said he learned about insider management buyouts from magazine articles and books including *How to Do a Leveraged Buyout or Acquisition.* [3]

Madsen's group also consulted over lunch with a neighbor and customer who had acquired a food processing plant in a management buyout from General Foods Corp.

"So we three fellows went over and had lunch with him one day and informally kicked around the things that they had been doing....It was a good experience for us to hear about the ups and downs.

"I always had the desire to run my own show," Madsen said. "I think that's kind of the ultimate challenge, as opposed to being a president of a division with an umbrella over you."

A Dead End

Back east, officials at Wang Laboratories in Lowell, Massachusetts, began to talk in 1981 about selling their software department so they could concentrate on their hardware systems.

Larry Munini, then head of Wang's software department, felt he had been dead-ended — handed a career cap.

Munini was not interested in being transferred into a Wang hardware division if his software division were sold. He was even less interested in starting a new business from scratch, something which seemed infinitely harder and more risky than buying his existing unit.

So Munini negotiated to buy the department from Wang and he

opened his own company, Genesys Software Systems, later that year in nearby Lawrence, Massachusetts.

Veteran retailer Jerry Gura was recruited by the Outlet Company of Providence, Rhode Island, in 1979 to do a turnaround on its chain of Cherry Webb & Touraine specialty apparel stores in New England.

"I was brought on board and given two alternatives in my contract," Gura said. "It was my role to turn the company around or improve the results so it would be salable. At that point I asked for and was granted right of first refusal."

In two short years, Gura and his management team did all of that. They turned the retail chain around. They made it salable. And, in 1982, they completed an insider buyout.

Considering Your Career Alternatives

It's time for contingency planning on your own account. You need to explore the alternatives, opportunities, hazards, and havens available to you in other situations.

Your career decisions will be complicated by a whole range of emotional, physical, psychological, and factual considerations involving you, your friends, and family.

One of the alternatives you have is identical to one mentioned earlier for your company: do nothing.

After reviewing your plans for yourself and your company, you could become convinced that things are not as bad as they first seemed. You could conclude that there is too much risk involved in starting over with a different company or launching your own business.

Or you could go the other way, decide that you do not want to suffer through another ten years of corporate life watching good friends hurt and sent away.

You could decide to make a move to improve your situation, to prepare a new career and investment portfolio for yourself.

We are not talking about a contingency plan for a loser, a plan for someone who missed his profit plan, someone whose days with the firm are already numbered.

You're a success. You have expertise. You are not ready to be dead-ended. You have alternatives.

You could accept a position with another firm, perhaps a competitor. The change of scene would remove the burden of the underproducing division from around your neck and give you a new career base to build upon.

Moving to another firm is a logical alternative. It would satisfy your basic compensation needs. It would be a safe move in your chosen field — corporate management. You selected corporation management as a career after graduation because it offered instant prestige and rich promises of training, experience, and, most important, business contacts. And, yes, the pay was good.

By the time you were thirty, the money and benefits seemed phenomenal. You enjoyed a great sense of upward mobility and permanency with the firm. You couldn't imagine ever breaking away from the corporation.

Since then, as you've risen in the ranks, you've had some problems with corporate politics and your misfit division. And you realize that you would run the risk of duplicating your current unsatisfactory circumstances in another corporation.

Many Alternatives

But looking for a management job elsewhere should remain an alternative if your career appears permanently stalled with your current employer. And if you can move into a more appropriate salary bracket elsewhere. And if your current job is taking its toll on your health, family, or personal life.

Another alternative would be to resign and use your contacts to become a business consultant in your special field.

Or you could go back to graduate business school and begin retraining for a new career or business.

Or you could put the corporate life and politics totally behind you, take a long holiday, meet with some realtors, and buy a country inn, ski lodge, or vacation ranch.

John Kenneth Galbraith, the economist and a summer resident of Vermont, said that state's economy was sustained by new residents who poured their life's savings into the renovation of old inns and then sold the works to new owners who poured their life's savings into renovating the renovations.

Wry comments from academe aside, the small business option would give you 100 percent independence to manage in your own way with a free rein to implement your own ideas.

There's nothing the matter with honestly assessing yourself as a corporate misfit and chucking it all for a gift shop or motel business if that's exactly what you and your family want to do. Frank Kirkpatrick left a successful but high-pressure job at Young and Rubicam, trading Madison Avenue for the J.J. Hapgood general store in Peru, Vermont (population 312). And he's happy.

However, anyone who has survived until near age forty as a corporate manager has a wealth of career alternatives beyond waiting on tourists or performing plumbing repairs.

We would hate to see you waste valuable managerial talent and experience simply because of a career impasse with one employer.

Time For Consideration

Now is the time for you to find a relaxed time and place — perhaps on vacation — to do some optimistic thinking and brainstorming about the desirabilities and feasibilities of your life.

Write a confidential report to yourself entitled "Personal Goals and Objectives." You've done it regularly for your company, now do it for yourself.

What are your goals, values, strengths, weaknesses, and needs?

Do you have a vision? Can you articulate your hopes? What do you do best? What do you want from life? What is the relationship you hold between work and life?

Do you work for a living? Or do you place equal emphasis on working and living? Or do you live for working?

Do you thrive within the corporate structure? Would you move anywhere to follow a corporate opportunity?

Or do you feel you have been stifled within the corporate environment? Do you crave independence? Would you quit your job before leaving your home and neighborhood?

Are you highly disciplined in use of time, money, materials, equipment, and labor? Do you see yourself successfully managing your division after a buyout?

What is your concept of wealth and how do you plan to achieve it? Would you be happy managing all your eggs in one basket or are you compelled to diversify your investments? Are you ready to pledge your home and personal assets as collateral in your insider buyout?

It is critically important for you to learn how to disclose yourself to others before you ask them to support your goals and serve on your behalf.

You will need to conceptualize and articulate your personal dreams and visions to yourself before you can transform them into statements of business goals and missions.

Of all the business decisions you have to make, deciding what you want to do for the rest of your life is the easiest.

The hard part is converting your wants into the action necessary to make it all happen.

The Insider Buyout

Just for fun, compare your division's problems to a college football game. Homecoming weekend. No score. Five minutes left to play.

Your team has the ball on its own twenty-yard line. Third down. Fifteen yards to go. And it's starting to snow.

A turnaround is when the coach sends in a new quarterback. A takeover is when the college president sends in a new coach.

An insider buyout is when your team fumbles the ball, you grab it, spot a hole in the line, and make it all the way to your opponent's five-yard line.

The insider buyout, like a recovered fumble, is an innovative solution to a team problem that frequently proves more productive for the team and the players than traditional solutions.

Even if you decide never to try an insider buyout, just knowing about this friendly, win-win business technique could be helpful to you in corporate decision-making or negotiating situations.

There are no published records of how many of the sales or divestitures of companies or their subsidiaries have been insider buyouts. Most of the insider buyouts are asset purchases too small to be noticed by the business journals. Many others, if noticed, are merely listed as divestitures or LBOs without indicating management's role.

However, this much is certain: the ways to conclude a successful insider buyout are as numerous as the number of insider buyouts concluded.

Several variations of insider buyouts have been pioneered by Tektronix, a Beaverton, Oregon, electronics manufacturer that encourages teams of employees to buy the technology it develops that the company cannot use. Then Tektronix provides mentoring and venture capital for the former employees' start-up companies which maintain close research and development ties to Tektronix.

General Electric also uses insider buyouts for its Technical Ventures group.

"When GE determines a new product will not fit its corporate strategy (e.g. expected volume too small), it offers to sell the technology, patents, and equipment to those managers who developed the product. GE also assists with financing and typically retains a 20 percent to 40 percent equity interest in the new company. In this way, GE stands to profit eventually from its investment in the project and provides an opportunity for entrepreneurial managers to run their own businesses," reports *Management Buyouts.* [4]

An equally strong example is the Minnesota Mining and Manufacturing Company, with its headquarters in St. Paul. 3M devotes 5.5 percent of its annual sales total to research and development. In many cases, this research has led to products that, for a variety of reasons, the corporation was not prepared to offer on the market. In many instances, 3M has encouraged entrepreneurism from within, creating and funding startup ventures from within and investing in its own management.

Don't Wait

We have detailed a few dozen insider buyouts in the pages that follow. Our hope is that you will avoid the plight of those who move too slowly towards their opportunity of a lifetime.

"What were your alternatives to an insider buyout?" we asked a heartbroken banker at a small, local Midwestern bank that structured an insider buyout — but too late to avoid being acquired by a large banking chain.

"We disappear," he said.

An insider buyout is for a manager who thinks business pressures and challenges are lots of fun, for whom business is an adventure and an avocation as well as a vocation.

The typical prospect for an insider buyout is a special breed, the blend of a career corporate manager and a small business entrepreneur. A manager who has performed well in the conformity of the corporate environment by keeping a strong streak of independence securely under control. But someone who has felt such control of independence has been stifling to innovation and decision-making.

To such a prospect, managing in a tightly controlled hierarchy he sometimes seems reduced from doing all the right things to doing all the wrong things right.

The IBO is a deal for someone who wants a vehicle for reaching the best of both worlds. Someone who will not be miserable without the perks and trappings of a large corporation. Someone who understands that an insider buyout will not solve all of life's problems.

Lou Auletta, who bought Bauer/Electro from a private owner in 1983, said this of insider buyouts: "It's the desire of most every general manager. They think, 'If it were mine, I'd be able to get more of the results of the effort.'

"It was something I've always wanted. The timing was right. We have four children. Our third is graduating in June. I felt I was at an age — forty-five — where I had to do something if I was going to do it."

Among the other things Auletta did at that important time in his life was to lose forty pounds.

"There's nothing like being able to take over something that you've been working with, something you have a good understanding of," Auletta said. "I had very little apprehension about doing it. I felt very confident in knowing the organization."

Consultants Nicholas Wallner and J. Terrence Greve cite "a strong desire" as the first characteristic of a successful company buyer. [4]

Other distinguishing traits they noted include a willingness to accept risk, persistence, patience, a sense of timing, and, finally, discipline in the use of time and other resources.

You have some of these qualifications. Plus, you are dissatisfied with your role of managing a misfit, underachieving division. And you have the management qualifications for running the division as a stand-alone enterprise.

But before you can finally determine whether an insider buyout is right for your corporation, you need to determine whether you and your family are right for an insider buyout.

If there is ever a time when you don't want to fool yourself, your advisors, or your lenders, it is now.

In an insider buyout, the manager is the biggest asset in the deal. If you do not fit — if you are not a durable asset — there will be no deal.

By now, you have reviewed the alternatives for you, your division, and the parent corporation.

It's time to select and implement the best alternative. Find the solution and seize the opportunity — for you and the firm.

An insider buyout, like a recovered fumble, could mean a fresh start for both the division and you. And the potential joys and rewards, like those in broken-field running, overshadow any risks that might be in the way.

Chapter III References:

[1] *Structuring and Financing Management Buyouts,* edited by L. Ryder Mason, Buyout Publications, Inc., San Diego.

[2] *Managing,* by Harold Geneen and Alvin Moscow, Doubleday & Co., 1984.

[3] *How to do a Leveraged Buyout or Acquisition,* by Nicholas Wallner and J. Terrence Greve, Buyout Publications, San Diego, 1982.

[4] *Management Buyouts* is one of a series of booklets published for clients by Ernst & Whinney.

Chapter IV

Positioning Yourself for an IBO

Money is not the biggest problem in an insider buyout. If your deal makes sense, you will have no trouble finding financing.

Your most difficult job in an insider buyout will be to reposition yourself.

You will need to develop a brand new set of relationships. New business connections. New career associations. New professional affiliations. New credit, supply, political, and regulatory relationships. And, yes, new and improved family relationships.

At the beginning, an insider buyout is a very lonely path leading to a very lonely decision point. You will be breaking management patterns, upsetting employment situations, changing people's lives, changing your personal relationships.

Can you stand being alone on this trail?

Many people considering an insider buyout would first study a wealth of books on such subjects as how to write a business plan, how to finance a new business, and how to structure a buyout. This makes sense, but there's a more important first step.

Forming Your Team

When your experience is limited and you don't have the time for prolonged study, we suggest that you put your first and best efforts into developing your own team of trusted business advisors to help you make important decisions. Not all at once, but one by one, building the best team you can.

This network of advisors will be essential before, during, and long after your insider buyout. It will be rewarding even if you decide not to change your career drastically.

The formula for management success in a small, independent business is centered around a versatile and independent owner-manager, a generalist who has the savvy to recruit the specialized skills needed from the ranks of independent, professional experts.

For starters, you'll need a good lawyer-negotiator. And a good tax and money man. And a creative deal-maker.

Personal and Family Relationships

If you quit your job and become an entrepreneur, your relationships with your family will change drastically.

As a trusted corporate official, you have been prudent about keeping the details of your employer's business affairs out of your personal and family life. Your life is essentially split between your office and your home.

But when you reposition yourself from a hired-manager to an owner-manager, you will want your family to be deeply involved in your business.

Talk with your family confidentially about your insider buyout from the very beginning.

Tell them about the risks and benefits. Talk with them about how changes in your business life could change their personal lives.

Perhaps not all members of your family will be enthusiastic. Some may fear they will have less independence and security with a "family business."

What will an insider buyout do to money set aside for college? Will there be time for family vacations? Will meal hours and weekends be impossible to plan? Does this mean somebody is going to have to give up riding or sailing?

At the very moment you are facing the biggest opportunity of your life, you do not want to find your home life, peace of mind, and family financial situation falling apart.

Your insider buyout will be revolutionary to your business relationships. You want it to be evolutionary, not revolutionary, to your family relationships.

John says that Martha, his wife, was a "good source of advice and inspiration because she lived through the thing with me and I kept talking to her. I wanted her to know what was going on so she would understand what we were going through, and, also, I respected her judgment and opinions, which were very helpful to me."

"They thought it was quite exciting," Tom Madsen said of the wives of the four partners who bought out Key Technology. "It was an adventure. It was scraping up nickels and dimes to put the thing together so it represented some financial risk to them. But I don't think any of them were that concerned because of our age and our track record."

"You need someone who is very supportive and extremely helpful, like my wife," Lou Auletta of Bauer/Electro said. "She generally works [at the business] two or three days a week on a part-time basis."

Auletta said he is also dependent upon his son, Louis Jr., a recent engineering school graduate. "I bounce a lot of things off him and I have a lot of respect for his recommendations. Even though the experience isn't there, the education and the understanding of the business are."

"There can't be any question that the spouses of all the principals were very instrumental in keeping us in the proper frame of mind during the eighteen months of acceptances and refusals, yeses and nos, gos and no-gos," Jerry Gura said of financing delays in his buyout of the CWT Specialty Stores.

"If there was anything life-sustaining during that period," he said, "it was the commitment of our four families to group behind the four principals. That was very meaningful. Relocations were a consideration. Children pulled out of schools. Homes to be sold, homes to be bought."

Talking about his wife, Dick Hug of Environmental Elements said, "To start with, she thought I was crazy. But after thinking about it, she said, 'We can do it. We can raise the finances. Why don't we do it?' She gave me that kind of encouragement."

Hug's son, 26, has degrees in marketing and finance. Hug said when he invited his son to join the business, the younger man's comment was, "It's one of the greatest compliments you've ever paid me."

Closer Family

"It's really brought our family closer together," Dick Snyder of Snyder General Corp said of his insider buyout. "All the kids want to know constantly what's happening. The business is a huge part of our life."

"You get a lot of peaks and valleys in this thing," Snyder said of an insider buyout. "You sometimes have difficulty getting the financial community to commit. They know you're trying to put together a group. But one lender won't commit because he doesn't want to be the first. And you go through a lot of peaks and valleys of emotion. There were times when I felt, 'Boy, this is just too much to do.'

"My wife kicked me in the butt a few times. She really challenged my ego, challenged my personal fortitude. She knew that I was never going to be happy until I ran my own business. While I worked very hard for public corporations, she knew that my long-term goal was this. If I didn't do this one, I probably wouldn't want to try another one because it's such a tremendous drain on energy and time. She was a real source of encouragement.

"And my kids! All three of them are in college. They were very supportive and also challenged me to continue and encouraged me to work at it harder."

Changing Business Relationships

Begin your search for business advisors the minute there is a possibility of leaving your employer corporation for an insider buyout or other new enterprise.

As the line-operations manager of a corporate division, you are not likely to be a hands-on expert in every area of finance, sales and marketing, production and manufacturing, business formation, or real estate acquisition. You are even less likely to be an expert in politics, public relations, government affairs, and the law.

You are accustomed to having people from all quarters of the corporate hierarchy provide you and your division with support services as specified by the corporate organization chart.

Also, there are extra dimensions and relationships within the corporate hierarchy from which you have received much unofficial support.

Help Is Lost

But the moment you walk out the door of your employer corporation, you will be leaving behind these comfortable professional and personal relationships that have provided you with both counsel and security.

"You'll be able to count your true business and corporate friends on three fingers, if you're lucky," said Bill Black of the New York-based McNamee Consulting Group, publishing specialists, when I chatted with him about my hopes.

How will you react when you reach out for familiar corporate supports that are no longer there?

How will you handle the corporate political pressures while planning and negotiating an insider buyout and at the same time doing your old job?

When you are the owner-manager, who will be on the lookout for you? Where will you find the grapevine? Who will give you instant feedback?

You need to master a new level of human relations as you leave the corporate environment of controlled and controlling relationships for a more free-wheeling and less predictable entrepreneurial environment of continuously changing human relationships.

You need to invest time and money in nurturing advisory relationships with your own support network of skilled, professional advisors and counselors who will help you make decisions.

This network is not the team of staff subordinates you hire to supervise and control your new company. It is a network of your most intimate and trusted advisors and counselors who are your peers and whose primary occupations are outside of your new company.

For counsel in our insider buyout of Garden Way Publishing, we had legal and accounting professionals, and we recruited help from three friends who are business consultants. Two have since joined our board of directors. Another remains an informal advisor.

For outside help, Dick Snyder turned to Dallas attorney Michael Caolo, who is now on the board of directors and general counsel for Snyder General Corporation.

"We have a very close personal friendship," Snyder said. "He's been my personal attorney for about ten years. He and I looked at several other deals during the 70s, but none of them came through....We spent every weekend for almost a year and many evenings [working on the buyout from Singer]. I would use vacation time to knock on doors [looking for financing] and he would be with me there. We were pretty inseparable at that time."

Bob Hagans, who took Unitog private in March, 1984, conceived that idea with investment banker G. Kenneth Baum while flying back to Kansas City from New York in August, 1983. (The pair serve on the board of directors of Sealright, of Fulton, New York, which left Phillips Corp. in a leveraged buyout.) Hagans and Baum met again in October, decided to go ahead with plans for a buyout, and within three weeks had secured $37 million in financing and packaged their buyout offer.

Jerry Gura credits Boston attorney Samuel "Sandy" Batcheldor of Goodwin, Proctor and Hoar for playing the vital supportive role in the CWT Specialty Stores buyout. "Sandy sat at our side during all the gos and no-gos. In terms of an outsider giving good support and advice, Sandy was the most important," Gura said of Batcheldor, who is now a CWT director and managing partner.

Doug Baker, a Vermont innkeeper, said, "Our most helpful business advisors were people who were in the business, people who had to do with the day-to-day operations.

"I started asking them [for advice] when we were still leasing. Nobody minded. I found that the people in the business are very helpful. They understood what it took....The helpfulness came very easily."

Baker also said prospective business owners could get much help from the members and staffs of state and national trade associations and from the instructors and attendees at business seminars.

When dealing with state agencies, Baker, a Vermont state senator, had one other suggestion: "Use your legislator. Ask for a letter of introduction before you meet with the regulators."

Lou Auletta of Bauer/Electro credited the idea for his buyout to discussions he began with a personal financial advisor: "We worked it out in breakfast meetings....I was looking towards a small investment. He was looking at it as a building block....'What do you have? What do you want to do? What are your retirement plans?'

"We wrote down goals. One of the goals I had was to become owner of a company. We had projected it for about a three- to five-year plan. It turned out that my opportunity came around sooner....He's someone you can discuss things with."

Building a New Support Network

The quality and quantity of support you need from your business support network goes way beyond the technical, problem-solving expertise of consultants and even beyond the recommendations of authoritative advisors.

We recommend you develop close, deliberative relationships with one or more trusted associates, who will become your counselors.

We use the term "counselors" not just in reference to lawyers but in its broader sense to include persons with whom you have special business advisory relationships, authoritative experts who are your advocates, confidants, and sponsors.

Your business counselors can be anyone who presents business alternatives to you in an advocacy relationship which is characterized by intense, intimate, and totally honest communications.

Your business counselors will not be mentors as the term is commonly used. "Mentor" implies a political and teaching relationship between a corporate veteran and someone on the fast track, a relationship dedicated to fostering success for and within an organization.

Your business counselors will not be your business partners. The role of a partner is to champion the partnership, not the other partners. Only in the rarest of partnerships — perhaps in a family situation — can business partners transcend business matters to counsel their partner selflessly.

Depending on their experience, your spouse, a relative, a neighbor, or a business associate could serve effectively as a business counselor. There may be friends you have kept at arm's length who are qualified and would be willing to serve as advisors if invited.

On the other hand, you can expect friends to give you only so much free time and expertise. You can go only so far preparing for an insider buyout without buying professional skills. You will need to identify the gaps and find the missing players.

Your Attorney

At the minimum, your team of business counselors needs to include a highly qualified attorney, a certified public accountant, and a lender to help organize the financing. Quite likely these professionals will not be the ones who are now handling your personal affairs.

Your relationship with your legal counsel is apt to be the closest and most prolonged. It will be your job to supply enough details about the players and the grand design of your deal so that your lawyer may make calculated judgments about the way the players are likely to behave and react.

Your Accountant

"I think a second fellow you need today is an astute tax accountant," said Victor Kiam. "With the tax laws the way they are, how you structure your deal financially is so important. You can structure it one way and pay a lot of taxes, or another way and not pay much taxes, and both ways are legal."

Your lawyer and accountant will be working for you as the legal and finance departments of your fledgling company. Their help will be needed in preparing or reviewing such instruments as the letter of intent to sell, asset inventories, auditors' reports, financial forecasts, financial statements, sale agreements, promissory notes, mortgage deeds, security agreements, release from liability agreements, lease transfers, non-compete contracts, and many other documents.

Your Relationships

Despite all the technicalities, your relationships with your professional business counselors in an insider buyout are likely to be very different from the traditional legal, accounting, or lending relationships.

Many professionals are experts in the technical aspects of law, accounting, taxation, or real estate and will be glad to prepare your paperwork. But they will make it clear that they are not dealmakers and are not in the business of helping people make up their minds about how to invest their time or money.

Do not be intimidated and diverted from finding true business counselors by these kinds of self-imposed limitations. These professionals may not trust their own business expertise. Or they may not trust business clients, and they may be concerned about their liability. Or there may be an unwritten, gentleman's agreement among professionals in your region to limit their practices to traditional, arm's-length relationships.

Keep looking for the talents and services you need, even if it means recruiting help from another region.

You want counselors who will go beyond the preparation of legal instruments and technical discussions about what you cannot do. You need counselors who will suggest your "should dos."

You will be looking for counselors who have ample experience with business clients and a good understanding of business rules of thumb. Counselors who will suggest different standards and alternatives for your comparison. Counselors who will look at a business deal in terms of the benefits versus the costs and the worst-case consequences. Counselors who will think of business, not as a necessary evil, but as an intellectually fascinating human endeavor.

You want counselors who will continuously review the financial plans for your new enterprise in terms of profits, losses, costs, prices, margins, and risks.

Similarly, you will want counselors who will continuously analyze your changing business relationships, looking for unfavorable consequences.

You want counselors whom you can implicitly trust, but who will also support their recommendations with data and legal references for you to review.

You want counselors who will engage in intense consultations about long-range strategy and decision making. Counselors you can call at home over the weekend and say, "Here's an idea. What do you think? Kick it around for a couple of days and get back to me Monday."

You might expect to pay more for professional business counseling than you would for ordinary assignments. But, in most cases, there should be no premium if the deal succeeds and no penalties if the deal fails. Your professional counselors deserve to be paid based solely on their time.

Although you will develop a close working relationship with each of your business counselors, it is not necessary or even desirable that you also develop close friendships with them.

Developing this relationship with your business counselors is going to take time. It's going to be a long getting-acquainted period with exchanges of information, followed by debates, agreements, or friendly disagreements over a minimum of a one- to two-year period.

Advice You Need

The advice you seek is not a list of instructions prepared for you by an expert, but a list of strategic alternatives developed jointly by you and your counselors, who are willing to coach you in decision-making.

After telling of the contribution of his wife, Tom Begel of Pullman Transportation said, "Personally, the best advice I got came from some good friends that I have who are still with the corporation but who weren't really a part of this transaction. If I had a problem I'd just sit down and say, 'What do you think about this? Am I being objective? Am I losing my perception?' "

In our Garden Way, Inc. deal, we'd turn regularly to Prescott Kelly, an entrepreneurial friend and former college classmate, now

president of the Stamp Collectors' Society in Redding, Connecticut.
On several occasions, I asked him, "Here's a problem that's
bothering me. You're objective, and you don't have a bias on the
subject. What do you think? Just how should I proceed?"

He'd give me straight talk on the phone for five minutes, and I'd
buy him a beer the next time I saw him. We probably had thirty
conversations, all at key times.

Lou Auletta's talks with his personal financial advisor led to the
Springfield, Massachusetts, investment banking firm of MacArthur/Nathan Associates whose partners eventually became involved in his buyout.

"We talk almost daily," Auletta said of investment banker Larry
R. Nathan, who is now Bauer/Electro's chief financial officer.
"There are many of the [management] things that he has taken over.
In addition to buying the business, we've formed a partnership and
are now in negotiations to buy the building.

"It's the kind of situation where we have a very comfortable
feeling with each other, the three of us [including investment banker
John R. MacArthur]. A year and a half ago, I didn't know them.
But we work well together and complement each other. We all have
our areas of expertise.

"There are many situations that come up that would be much
more difficult if I did not have those types of partners and people to
turn to."

Finding Your Business Advisors

The idea of building a support network of personal business
advisors outside your company may at first seem frivolous and
risky.

Previously you may have shunned close personal relationships,
believing them to be improper, imprudent, or a sign of weakness.
You may have preferred to be strongly independent. Or perhaps you
may have wanted to spare your friends the burden of your concerns,
or maybe it was simply a matter of not taking the time.

Probably you'll have to start from scratch in recruiting your informal group of advisors.

It's an important step. The inclination to seek help and be receptive to advice from a broad range of friends and associates may be the key to successful buyouts.

You will be looking for counselors, both professional and lay persons, who sincerely care about you and will not flavor their advice with hidden motives.

Although you may welcome advice from friends who are qualified to be your business counselors, don't ask them for it. Tell them about your proposed goals and visions and merely ask them for their comments. Many people you respect will not give you advice even if you ask. They may reply with factual statements. They may offer ritualistic or frivolous answers, or they may end the discussion by changing the subject.

Some people will not give advice because they do not want to become burdened with other people's problems or involved with their dreams. Some may fear rejection. Some may fear blame. Some may lack confidence in themselves — or you. Others may simply not have the time or patience.

Get Recommendations

Finding the professional business counselors you need is best approached by asking for recommendations from your business connections and from trusted professionals in related fields.

Call your most likely candidates and ask for introductory interviews with no commitment to retain. You might request that the initial interview be without charge, or you might offer to pay the basic rate for one or two hours.

Meet with your professional candidates one at a time in relaxed, uninterrupted privacy to discuss some of your basic goals and dreams. Encourage a free-flowing discussion of your business and personal goals and philosophies to see if there is a good fit and a possibility of a lasting relationship. But limit the discussion of your plans and needs until you are sure the relationship is right.

You will be looking for counselors who are skilled at communications and share the same enthusiasm for life and business with you.

Should Be Curious

The counselors you want will be very curious, not stand-offish, even during your initial interview. They should be interested in the history of your business problems and have questions about the steps you have taken to prevent a recurrence.

You will know, during that first meeting, that the relationship with a prospective counselor fits if you can make your visions come alive and if you are both open to the possibility that these visions can play a role.

You don't want to pay counselors to tell you to change your goals because they're too risky. You want their advice on your options for reducing, avoiding, isolating, or eliminating the risks. You want their help in changing your plans, not your goals.

You are trying to find one or more counselors who will support you in intimate decision-making discussions. You are searching for a relationship that will protect the objective and independent judgment for both parties.

Do not underestimate your ability to design and manage a suitable buyout plan. And do not let expert advisors downgrade the value of your manager's sense of business savvy.

Professional business counselors deal with specialized knowledge from the perspectives of craftsmen. They are unlikely to conceive of the insider buyout deal in a way that will be suitable to your instincts and goals.

You do not want a lawyer's deal. Or an accountant's deal. Or a banker's deal. You want a deal you can live with, a manager's deal.

Your Relationship

Well-qualified advisors will, of course, be well paid but the client-professional relationship is an employer-employee relationship. You pay, they perform for you.

You need to make it clear that you will control the thrust and direction of your insider buyout.

We asked our contributors how they found the advisors and counselors they needed to help with an insider buyout.

"Word of mouth. You call your friends," John Jordan of the

Jordan Company said. "That's where the best investment advice comes from. You make contacts. That's the way the whole business world works."

Larry Munini of Genesys explained how he finally found the right attorney. "Early on in my series of phone calls [seeking advisors], I called a neighbor who was an attorney. I gave him my spiel about how I was going to start this company. Would he like to put in money?

"He said, 'No, but I have all sorts of clients, all sorts of private investors who do this all the time. I'll introduce you.'

"I said, 'I need an attorney to represent me. Will you do that?'

"He said, 'Gee, that would be a conflict of interest if I were representing an investor. Let me give you the name of a buddy who lives across town.'

"Basically he put me in touch with the gentleman who ultimately wound up as my attorney — a very fortunate pass-along because that attorney turned out to be my most valuable advisor over the next six months."

Munini said his attorney and his venture capitalist serve on Genesys's board of directors. The attorney is also corporate counsel, a job that takes about one day a week.

Dick Hug said, "I decided that I was going to be with the very best law firm and the very best accounting firm that I could find. I engaged Arthur Anderson [the accounting firm] whose managing partner [a lawyer] I had known for a number of years here in Baltimore. He has come to work as my partner, executive vice president, and chief financial officer of the company. I also engaged Basher and Howard, the number one law firm in Baltimore. Both of them were crucial to making this deal go."

Victor Kiam said the key to selecting advisors is looking for someone with a successful business track record you respect.

Kiam said one of his advisors is comptroller of a large company. They met through a mutual friend. "We became friends because I liked him. He gave me a new dimension. I could throw out, 'What do you think about this or that? What do you think of the financial situation six months from now?' We developed a friendship, played tennis together. After the tennis we sat and chit-chatted. But you've got to respect the advice. Some people try to get too much advice. You have to select those individuals whom you respect, then go to them. If you start going around asking twenty-five people for their advice, you're going to find you have twenty-five answers and you won't know what the hell to do."

"I don't know any business today that can exist without a lawyer," Kiam said. "But the worst thing you can do is to go to a very big law firm because you have a friend there who is a managing partner. You've got a little, dinky business. So he gives it to a trainee. I'd rather go to a smaller firm where the brains of the firm will give you the time to which you're entitled."

Listening to Your Counselors

Judgments must be made and decisions must be risked.

Now is the time to take your lists of goals and alternatives for your business and personal life and sit in intense and intimate discussions with your personal business counselors.

Is your vision of an insider buyout capable of execution? Can it pass the test of critical analysis by these counselors? Can you make your vision come alive in communications with your potential financial supporters?

This creative advisory process begins with a complete exchange and acceptance of facts, ideas, opinions, and feelings.

There needs to be shared definitions, trust, and near perfect communications between you and your business counselors if they are to help you reach your goals.

If you, the business manager, are not articulate in explaining your goals, you will not get much out of the relationship. You need to be explicit in telling them your motives, goals, and dissatisfactions. Put the issues out on the table, not as uncertainties but as concrete proposals which can serve as marching orders to the counselors.

You need to learn to ask your advisors the penetrating questions that will elicit the perceptive points of view that no computer printout will provide.

Listening Important

Listening is the key to the counseling. For the relationship to be successful, both the client and the counselor need to want to listen to each other, not just to hear words and understand their meaning, but to comprehend clearly what is intended by the conversation. They need to listen and observe each other quietly without interruption, criticism, or distracting body language. During the listening, questions are asked only as a test for understanding, not as the occasion to begin a rebuttal.

The counselor is listening in quiet analysis, searching for lapses in the client's logic. Similarly, your purpose in listening is to gain new perspectives, not to win political points, defend yourself, or win an argument.

Listening is a process, a tool, a critical skill, and an art. It's probably the start of communications.

The listening must have a beginning and an end. At some point, after pleasantries have been exchanged, and everyone has secured his or her notepad, briefcase, and coffee, the conversation and listening begins. Comments are withheld until the listening is over and it is time to switch to a feedback phase and the other party's time to listen. Break times and conclusions should be so designated without attempting to continue the talks while walking on out into the parking lot.

In our deal for Garden Way Publishing, I had to learn to listen more carefully than ever before. Frankly, I used to do more talking than listening, and this was an important habit to change.

Meeting Times

The best time to meet with your business counselors is at your mutual convenience. Frequently this will be outside of office hours, such as Friday evenings after work or Sunday evenings, and away from the office. Lunch hour may not allow enough time. A long dinner in a corner booth at an uncrowded restaurant will be better. It's a matter of getting out from behind your desk and letting your defenses down with someone you can trust.

It is a good technique to meet occasionally with two or more advisors by way of coalescing their collective wisdom and arriving at a consensus. However, do not try to bring together advisors who have conflicting personalities or points of view.

You are looking for creative alternatives and you may need to make a judicious compromise in reaching a solution. You do not need to mediate an argument in the process.

In the end, the effectiveness of your business counselors will be conditioned by the degree of authority you give them.

Alter Egos

Ideally, your business counselors will go beyond trust and professional qualifications to provide another dimension to the relationship. They will be your alter egos — your other identities.

Alter egos are your anchors, your port in the storm. You share time, space, and identity with your alter egos. The relationships are nurtured by such factors as background, special training, and shared experiences in your business dealings.

The toughest struggle in the business counseling relationship is removing the barriers to complete communication yet remaining fiercely independent. Intimacy must not mean loss of independence, judgment, or objectivity.

Counselors and clients need to be comfortable enough with each other to say they think the other one is crazy.

Happily, when the creative business counseling relationship is made to work, the success will not be limited to your business. The effects will go way beyond business success to benefit every aspect of your life.

"I got a lot of that kind of encouragement from the Arthur Anderson Company and the managing partner who has since gone into my business as a partner," Dick Hug said. "He's very creative. Very innovative. And as legal counsel, he gave me all sorts of encouragement. 'Hey, we can do this.' He gave me a good structure for the business. He was really key in putting the entire transaction together.

"This was roll up the shirtsleeves. I would get calls literally at two o'clock in the morning from either my accounting people or attorneys. Saturdays, Sundays, what have you. It was a round-the-clock situation for sixty days.

"We developed a very close personal friendship, much more than a business relationship, with the accountants and attorneys who were working on the case.

"They're sort of rooting for the little guy buying the company from the big guy, that's the thing that developed. It's an experience I'll never forget."

Chapter V

The IBO Alternative

You have completed your study of the three alternative moves for your division, as outlined in Chapter III. Do any of them look like good moves, ones that will benefit your parent company?

If your answer is an unqualified yes, your next move, of course, must be to report that to those who named you to make a study and recommendations.

If your answer is no, you have more work to do.

It is our experience that each of the alternatives — divestiture, turnaround, and liquidation — offers real promise when first considered. Then further study reveals flaws or problems.

Divestiture sounds so neat and clean — until you think of lengthy get-acquainted sessions, lengthier negotiations, the baring of both division and corporation secrets, the loss of productive hours during all this time, the possibility of failure to reach an agreement.

Turnaround sounds so hopeful — but you've really turned over every stone before and are no closer to solving the division's problems, no nearer to making the division fit with the rest of the corporation. And would there be any support from headquarters if this were recommended?

Liquidation sounds so clear-cut — and it is. It rapidly becomes apparent that you would lose money — bundles of money — and find yourselves heir to public relations problems that just won't go away. It means the company will accept perhaps 10¢ to 50¢ on balance sheet items such as inventory and receivables.

Despite these negative conclusions, your study has been productive. You have learned what won't work. You've also become aware that in any move that you make, you must be sure not to create problems that could be even worse than those you now have. And you've learned techniques to use in testing other alternatives.

The person who has read this book thus far will not be surprised when we suggest that there is yet another alternative for the ills of your ailing division —the insider buyout.

That same person should not be surprised when we recommend a thorough study to determine whether this alternative promises real benefits for both you and your corporation — not just you, the eager buyer, but also your corporation, for whom you're conducting this study and are making recommendations.

Your analysis must be brutally honest. Its goal: to evaluate what exists so that you can determine accurately what could be.

It is much the same type of analysis that outsiders would have made had your corporation elected to sell the division. But there is one major difference: you, as manager, should know most of the answers and in a depth that only a division manager can know them.

When you have finished this evaluation, you should have answers to these questions:

1. Why is the division an underachiever? You know many reasons, but look again. What assumptions did you make as a corporate manager? Are those assumptions still appropriate? And would they be if the corporate infrastructure no longer existed?

2. What costs, specifically, can be eliminated? You are looking particularly for ways to reduce general services and administrative expenses. No doubt, you, as division head, are paying each month for your share of headquarters services and personnel. Could some of these expenses be cut if you bought out the division? Could some be eliminated?

3. What decisions did you make that were disastrous? Could they be reversed? What decisions added unproductive cost? Could those costs be eliminated now? Be honest. Your answer need be seen by no one but you.

4. Can the payroll be cut? Have you hired anyone whom you didn't need? Who remains on the payroll because of a personal friendship with you or one of your superiors?

(Note that you are looking for *your* mistakes in these first four questions. You may be able to blame others now for some of these mistakes, but if you do an IBO, there will be no one else to blame.)

5. What assets are indispensable to this operation? Make lists of:
Key personnel
Operating assets
Product names or trademarks

The most important item on these lists may be the product name or trademark. You, the insider, may be one of the few people your corporation will trust with a license to use that name. And the name may be of critical importance to you if you are to keep sales at existing levels and maintain current distribution levels.

6. What assets can you do without? Again, make lists of:
Personnel
Operating assets
Other assets

Here is an opportunity to pinpoint where operating costs can be cut and where extraneous assets can be identified, then either not purchased in the IBO or sold soon after completion of the deal.

7. What business relationships would be threatened by this move? Could the division, if it became your company, survive the loss?

Diagnosing Your Division

The evaluation process you will use is little different from what you have been doing for both your division and the parent company.

A classic example of a manager who found his division in distress, diagnosed the problem, assessed his alternatives, and developed a recovery plan is David Houck, the veteran superintendent at U.S. Steel's McDonald Works in McDonald, Ohio.

Houck's success story begins in 1979, a time of massive steel industry plant closings and worker layoffs. [1]

Houck was asked by company officials to draft a plan to minimize the closing of more mills and the loss of more jobs. He studied the company's strengths, weaknesses, and prospects for four months.

Houck recommended that U.S. Steel close its Ohio Works in Youngstown and retrofit the McDonald Works with an electric furnace and caster costing $208 million. But Houck's reprieve plan went to the U.S. Steel headquarters in Pittsburgh in November, 1979, one week before the company announced it was ceasing operations in Youngstown in a move to stem mounting operating losses and capital outlays.

Convinced after four months' study that cutbacks in labor coupled with increased productivity could save one of the McDonald mills, Houck kept playing with the numbers in his plan.

For $3 million in operating capital, Houck figured he could keep one specialty mill running at the McDonald Works with a start-up crew of twenty-five.

Thanks to backing by a local venture capital company, plus long-term lease and $3 million in plant improvements by U.S. Steel, Houck opened McDonald Steel Corp. in September, 1980. He retains a 2 percent equity in the new company.

Steel began rolling out of the McDonald mill a year later. By 1984, Houck had opened a second mill and increased employment to about 125.

Like Houck, you need to determine exactly what has caused your misfit division to have such a poor record. Name the situations. Name the sins. Name the sinners. And if the shoe begins to pinch, look in the mirror. Be specific about your own role in the misfit.

Has there been a lacking of funding and tender, loving care from headquarters?

Have there been problems with headquarters involving indecision, delay, and a mismatch of controls?

Has your division been hindered and made less productive by conformance to the corporate culture?

Is there a basic conflict on objectives between the division and the parent corporation?

What decisions did you make that led to problems? Financial mistakes? Production mistakes? Errors in forecasting?

What were your faulty assumptions? Have you cut corners on planning? Have you shown poor judgment with people?

After you have diagnosed your division's problems and pinpointed the blame, you are ready to move on to selecting the cure.

It is important that you keep proceeding patiently step by step through this long planning process from the earliest moments that you sense an insider buyout might be feasible.

What If You Owned the Business?

Your next exercise is to imagine the division under ideal circumstances as a stand-alone, privately owned company with you as the owner and the chief executive officer.

Don't worry about how you will get from here to there. Simply imagine that process completed for the next set of "what ifs."

You have at your fingertips for reference a full array of your division's completed management plans. They include the long-range plan, the finance plan, the contingency plan, and a marketing plan.

Plus, as suggested in Chapter III, you have a Manager's Best-Case Scenario. This is an important scenario in which you envision managing the division under ideal circumstances.

Then in Chapter IV you discussed with your advisors and counselors your personal goals and objectives.

Now is the time to begin preparation of your Buyout Feasibility Study.

This will be a realistic review and reshaping of all of your pertinent corporate plans and reports as if your division were divested from the corporation and reestablished as an independent business.

How would a buyout affect the corporation's finances?

How would it affect the corporation's long-range plans?

Would the pullout of your division have an adverse impact on the corporation's remaining product mix and marketing plans?

Remember, the solutions to your problems at the division level are not necessarily solutions to problems for the parent corporation. But it is essential that problems be solved at both headquarters and the division if an insider buyout is to be concluded and eventually be successful.

If your early studies of the impact of a buyout show the deal would not solve problems for headquarters, forget about your dreams for an insider buyout and look for yet another alternative.

But, assuming you are still on a win-win track, ask yourself if your management mistakes with your division would be reversed or reduced if your division were reshaped overnight into a stand-alone company. Or would they linger to haunt you?

Would your good assumptions still be appropriate if the corporate infrastructure no longer existed?

What Changes?

Your task here is to consider how the historic or existing problems with your division would be reshaped if somehow your division were transformed into an autonomous business.

Here are some areas to consider, and, if you give it some thought, you may add as many more for your own list:

• Your division's top priorities.

• The change in them if the support of the corporate structure is lost.

• The cash flow.

• Any chronic accounts-receivable problems that might cripple a new company.

• Warehouse space.

• Garaging and maintaining company vehicles.

• Possible legal and financial threats caused by pulling your division out of the corporation.

• Public-relations problems.

• Political problems.

• Employee unrest and labor union difficulties.

• Possible ways to cut costs — the payroll, distribution, less research, others.

• Overhead that can be eliminated because demands of headquarters no longer exist.

• Overhead that must be created with the loss of the corporate backing, in such areas as the comptroller's office, the personnel office, the customer service department.

• Reorganization for long-term effectiveness and creativity.

• Ways to better serve your customers.

• Greater employee commitment, productivity, and fulfillment.

• Better allocation of resources.

• Improved methods of procurement.

• Methods of attracting and holding the best managers and other employees.

Suddenly you begin to paint the picture of how well your division could perform if driven by an entrepreneur with a long-term vision of the operation at its best.

The energy comes from your identification and commitment with your division. After all, it's your business.

But remember, you are working on your Buyout Feasibility Study. You are concerned in this exercise not with desirabilities, but with probabilities and capabilities.

'Be Realistic'

"Be realistic," advised John Jordan of The Jordan Company. "A lot of managers who have bought their divisions have ended up in bankruptcy.

"It happens all the time. They read stories about guys buying their own divisions, and they get the idea they would like to buy theirs. They believe, all of a sudden, something wonderful is going to happen. Sometimes it does, sometimes it doesn't.

"The biggest problem, especially in the large divisions, is the division presidents have delegated everything to subordinates. After the buyout, they've got to go back to work and handle a big workload. Sometimes they're in for a rude awakening.

"They've been romanced by the illusion of grandeur. It's kind of a sad thing in many cases.

"What are the pitfalls? They are not good managers. Or they are in a dying business that nothing can save.

"Some managers have a tendency to do a buyout with a flair and a touch of drama to improve their negotiating position. And then they end up overfinancing and overleveraging and get in trouble. This works to the benefit of the seller more often than not.

"On the other side of the coin, there are the inefficient operations that are substantially improved when they get into the hands of entrepreneurs.

"You have to be realistic about how talented you think you are," Jordan said.

Our Buyout

In our buyout of Garden Way Publishing, we believed that our book line was improving in terms of quality and new ideas.

Headquarters also believed our books were getting better. But they showed only lukewarm interest in our line and were not highly supportive or understanding of our division's unique problems. In a company where the overwhelming percentage of sales and profits were coming from manufacturing, that should not have been a surprise to anyone. Within the corporation, our publishing division was a no-fit.

We took a lot of good-natured joking within the divisions about some of our bread-and-butter titles, for example *The Family Cow* or *Raising Pigs.*

The pacesetter in the corporation — and in the garden industry — is the Troy-Bilt Roto Tiller - Power Composter. This is the famous "Big Red" tiller that can dig up turf and still be controlled with only one hand.

The tillers are manufactured by modern assembly-line techniques at a historic brick factory complex in Troy, New York. Three generations of some families have worked for the corporation.

Obviously, the tiller plant thrives on a different type of corporate manufacturing culture and sophisticated manufacturing management than was workable in our publishing division. The line of tillers ranges from 125 to 330 pounds and sells for $500 to $1700 per unit. By contrast, in publishing, our average retail orders range from two ounces to two pounds and sell for $1.95 to $50.

Friends of ours who transferred within the corporation from tillers into the retail or publishing divisions — from manufacturing to service — found a different world. It was like a career change.

They had been accustomed to the support a large company can provide: mainframe computers, state-of-the-art telephone-intercom systems, management seminars, and regional sales meetings. In the publishing division, people carried in their own chairs and coffee and held conferences around a ping pong table with hand-held calculators.

Everyone on the board of directors recognized that our publishing division, no matter what its potential, would remain a misfit within the corporate structure.

A turnaround try was under way, but the key players kept running into difficulties.

Headquarters had few acceptable alternatives. They could sell the division — possibly to another publishing firm. But this would allow the buyer to use the Garden Way name which headquarters understandably wanted to control. The sale to an outside buyer would also require many months of negotiations when they wanted a quick, clean break.

Liquidation would mean an unacceptably low redemption value for the assets.

It was at this point, early spring 1983, that we suggested our plan for an insider buyout. We had all known each other and expected negotiations to be friendly. We had all worked together on the finances of the division, so there would be no disagreement as to the validity of the numbers or values. And most important, our proposal meant the negotiations would be speedy and a deal would be closed quickly.

Our Study

Despite our confidence, we conducted a very realistic and, we thought, conservative feasibility study on the proposed buyout before making our offer. This included our editorial prospectus, a marketing plan, and a full set of financial estimates.

The national economic outlook was bright and interest rates were falling. On the other hand, we were concerned that as business got better, people who were natural book buyers and readers might well leave their armchairs and fly to Paris, go water skiing in Florida, or, at the least, go out for dinner and the evening more than in the counter-cyclical period.

Realistically, we felt we could thrive in both good and bad economic times. We believed we could find ways to cut costs and build sales to more than make up for the risks we were taking. New and non-traditional sources of revenue were identified, cost reductions detailed, and a totally new distribution arrangement was outlined. Missionary spending of marketing money, seen as beneficial to the overall promotion of the corporation and all of its divisions, products, and services, would be eliminated.

Our primary reasoning behind our insider buyout was not so much a dream of creating new lines of books — which we are doing — as it was a chance to consolidate the company's administration and fine-tune its marketing.

We were able to project savings of nearly $500,000. That is a big chunk of savings in our little business, enough to convince us that an insider buyout was not only feasible, but the only practical thing to do.

What's the Potential?

Victor Kiam of Remington Products said, "My whole outlook towards the feasibility of a business buyout is the potential. I wouldn't recommend the move to acquire unless there was a potential to do something with this dying albatross.

"I'd much rather buy a small company that I could improve than take a company that earns $10 million and after ten years still makes $10 million.

"I'd make damn well sure that there was an opportunity for growth."

The Exception

Of course, there is an exception to every rule. Larry Munini of Genesys Software Systems seems to be the exception to the rule of performing a thorough buyout feasibility study before making an offer.

"Our product is software packages for IBM computers, and

Wang is a competitor of IBM in the manufacture of computers. Our department was obviously outside the mainstream of Wang's primary business."

When Munini saw a memo suggesting that his software department be sold, he talked about the proposed divestiture with his wife and a few people who reported to him. But he did not discuss the problem with any outside counselors.

"About a week later there was a meeting called in Dr. Wang's office to study the problem. There were about fifteen to twenty people around the conference table. Dr. Wang said, 'Shall we sell it?' Somebody piped up, 'Sure,' and a bunch of reasons were offered.

"Anybody who knew anything knew that the studying was over: the decision had been made....It was a fait accompli.

"Somebody said, 'How much can we get for it?' The number of $20 million was suggested. Someone mentioned a company that had just completed a public offering and was flush with cash.

"They asked me if I wanted to be a member of a committee of two to meet with the prospect. I very quickly declined.

"Dr. Wang made a comment, 'Yes, you're too close to it. You wouldn't want to be involved in that.'

"Wang has its own culture which we called the 'Wang Way.' The unspoken word on the tip of everybody's tongue is the loyalty to the company. Nobody had ever left the company to go with the product. It was an unspeakable consideration. I had been there for sixteen years. It was unsaid, but the thought was, 'Why would I ever want to leave the company when I would be offered a transfer within the company?'

"The meeting ended. I went out in the hallway and did a U-turn. I came back in and had a two-minute meeting alone with Dr. Wang. I said I'd like to start a company and buy the product from him.

"He said, 'I understand why you declined to be on the negotiating committee,' I said, 'You betcha.' "

"I had the feeling I could do it," Munini said. "I was the product manager while it was at Wang and felt it wasn't going to be that much different. I had the internal self-confidence that we could make a real money-making process out of it. There was never any doubt in my mind that if I could get it out the door, I could make a go of it. It was not something I did research on.

"When opportunity strikes, you have to make a decision either to go or no go."

Envisioning an Insider Buyout

"Vision is a critical tool in creating the future of your organization the way you want it to be....It actually sets the context to your business plan and makes its implementation a high probability event."

This from business consultant Patricia Passmore McKeon. [2]

"Vision appeals to people's highest aspirations....A vision is not just a wish list; it embodies what is most important to people....

"Vision gives meaning to work. First, vision inspires people to create rather than to react or respond....

"Secondly, it is not enough to have a vision. Somehow, it has to be articulated. Personal example is a powerful means of showing people 'how we do business around here....'

"Sometimes people have difficulty articulating their vision because it would mean talking about feelings or 'idealistic stuff....'

"Vision is about leadership in an ambiguous future. It is a guide through uncharted waters. Vision is the heart of creating your organization and the results you want. It is indeed a very practical tool," McKeon concluded.

Your job as a manager is to manage change in moving you and the division from here to there. Good management begins with a clear vision of distant goals.

Now is the time for mapping new goals — the creative, friendly, win-win solutions to the problems of your division, the parent company, and your management career.

Ask yourself, "If I could do it all over, what would I have done to improve the management?"

In your search for vision, be willing to suspend your beliefs in the limitations of time, space, human resources, and money.

Think of your division once again, this time in fresh, visionary terms as a restructured, reborn, autonomous company. Go beyond actualities to imagine a wide range of possibilities. Go beyond feasibilities to dream about desirabilities.

Then, before it vanishes, capture and record the essence of your vision. Call this your Entrepreneur's Best-Case Scenario.

Are you able to see yourself clearly in control of this business?

Would this transformation permit a faster growing, stronger business?

Remember, you are concerned here with your vision, not your business plan. You are not ready at this early stage in a buyout to do a detailed business plan. Before you begin to assemble any concrete numbers, before you begin any dealing, first you need to have a vision of the deal.

Your vision is not something that is set in type and bound in a binder. You have notes and a broad-brush picture of your vision, but you cannot quite take the measurements yet.

Your vision, your Entrepreneur's Best-Case Scenario, is a picture of a time and place when things are better. When shared with your colleagues, your vision will be the power that fuels your insider buyout.

Your Insider Buyout Plan

It is time to begin a rough draft of an Insider Buyout Plan.

This will be adding a bit more concrete to your vision of what it is that you propose to buy.

This is still not your New Business Plan — the specifics of what you do with the business after you own it.

You have not yet determined exactly what it is you are going to buy.

This is a transition plan: how you plan to manage the insider buyout transaction. How you plan to structure the deal. How the transaction will immediately transform the business. And what the overall mission and strategy of the new independent business will be.

You are studying the appropriateness of a particular type of deal — the insider buyout — to your particular division.

This is a first draft of your eventual business plan which will be treated in Chapter IX when financing becomes the focus.

Meanwhile, you proceed with your Insider Buyout Plan, using any of the same planning guides or division report formats that you have been using in the earlier diagnostic and prescriptive exercises.

A rough draft of an Insider Buyout Plan may be a pile of notes or an integrated plan on computer files.

Your Insider Buyout Plan should specify exactly what problems the divestiture/acquisition is intended to solve.

Your task here is to look beyond the historic or existing problems with your division to see the "what ifs" of an insider buyout transaction.

Is there a growing niche in a big market for your division/company's products and services? What will be your new competitive position? Do you have a business sense of a marketing parade underway, with your division left standing on the sidelines? Would an insider buyout help you lead your company in a race to get out ahead of that parade?

When Genesys Software Systems was still a department of Wang, sales were handled by the Wang's hardware sales force, and the biggest source of new business was word-of-mouth. Once separated, Larry Munini was able to organize his own marketing department of software specialists.

In the insider buyout of CWT Specialty Stores, Jerry Gura said, "We were able to attract some very talented people who did not want to be working for the subsidiary of a non-retailing company.

"We began opening new stores, on which there had been an embargo.

"We were able to internally capitalize the necessary and needed remodeling of a number of stores that had been neglected.

"And we were able to dramatically change the merchandising posture of the company by dropping certain divisions that contributed considerable revenue but not much profit. This is one of the things you don't do when you are reporting to a public company that is expecting you to increase sales."

Getting Positive

Gradually, as your vision coalesces, you begin to drift away from the negative connotations of past and existing problems into the positive language of creative action, future solutions, and mutual success.

Do you sense that in your division you have something that is likely to grow and become robust with the right mix of time, and energy?

Does your Insider Buyout Plan — your pile of notes — suggest how and when you will provide and harness that energy?

You are keeping both eyes on the future as you steer your division away from the shoals of past mistakes.

You are not letting yourself become preoccupied with bailing out the boat. You are exploring for passages to the New World.

You are creatively looking at your problems from every conceivable angle. You are mentally sailing around the world and coming back to see your problems from a different direction, with a rising sun instead of a setting sun.

Qualifying Your Division for an IBO

As the inside manager you have diagnosed the problems with your misfit corporate division. You have identified the insider buyout as a feasible cure, and this has led to your vision of a rebirth. And so you have begun to draft your Insider Buyout Plan, your prescription for the transition.

Now, at this challenging moment when you are considering buying your employer's business, take a step back and look at your division from the perspective of an outsider.

You may have some valuable advantages in an insider buyout that no outsider can approach. You may be the only one the company would trust with a license to use the corporate goodwill, trademark, or logos traditionally used in your division.

The product tradename may be of critical marketing importance. You will need to rely immediately on the existing sales outlets, distribution networks, and customer base before you have time to establish your own new company identity.

For example, in our buyout of Garden Way Publishing, we bought the inventory and rights to distribute, sell, and republish existing Garden Way Publishing books. We were also licensed to continue using the name Garden Way Publishing for new titles while we gradually grew into new identities.

Your BBD

This is a great time to do what I called a Brief Business Description, where you detail twenty to twenty-five key points about the business, everything from product description to the future of the industry. This is our BBD.

Brief Business Description

Products: Garden Way's quality trade paperback books, hardcover books, bulletins, and advertising card "marketplaces."

Services: Supplies editorial packaging to Garden Way under contract.

Employees: 14

Location: Publishing and editorial offices, Bennington, Vermont. Customer service, warehousing and distribution, Charlotte, Vermont.

Production: Subcontracted to major printers.

Distribution: Direct to the consumer by mail order; indirectly, to the trade and special markets, through commissioned sales representatives.

Strengths: Name, image, lists, editorial niche, advertising sales capacity, with 12-year history and roots going back 40 years. Quality product, high degree of customer satisfaction, experienced management.

Weaknesses: Transitional situation, product packaging.

Strategy: Growth in, and into, high potential publishing areas.

Ownership: M. John and Martha M. Storey, 95 percent. Key employees, 5 percent.

Scope: Producing and selling editorial material to numerous consumer markets.

Key Statistics: Revenues $3MM, profit $30M, assets $450M. Anticipate $3.9MM in 1984 revenues, with profitability.

Industry Definition: Publishing, through mail order, trade, and special channels.

Customer Group: "Country living" readers and consumers, affluent and exurban.

Need Served: Do-it-yourself information, plans, and dreams for country life.

Technology: Printing and paper.

Industry Size: Multi-segmented $7.6 billion. Quality trade segment $350 million. Growth anticipated in latter segment at above average levels between 1984 and 86.

Factors Affecting Growth: Disposable income up, population shifts to country up, housing starts up, growth in gardening and self-sufficiency, do-it-yourself interest up.

Product Vulnerability: Cheaper books, data base publishing, TV and home entertainment.

Product Breadth: Extensive, 150 titles. Five major subject categories.

Barriers to Entry: Capital, and development of image, name, list.

Technology: None currently. Will look to electronic and data base publishing as those industries emerge.

Integration: Limited. Will explore greater control of editorial production and eventually printing.

Printing: All subcontracted, avoiding large investments in plant and equipment at this time.

Profitability: Modest currently. Eight percent by 1986. Objective:10 percent plus.

Channels of Distribution: Mail, trade, special, foreign, premium.

Prices: Average $8.95. Increasing.

Terms - Conditions: Trade and special, 60–90 days. Varies by segment.

Imports: Non-competitive. Source of raw product.

Seasonality: Spring, fall strength.

Competitors: Lane (Sunset), HP Books, Ortho, Rodale.

Your Relationships

You begin to look immediately at how your buyout will affect relationships with certain people and firms. Some indispensable relationships will need to be preserved at all costs. Others may be threatened by a buyout but may not be considered essential to your ultimate success.

In a highly leveraged deal, you will be looking for modest and steady growth potential — but not runaway growth which would strain your needs for capital in leveraged deal and could lead to an early shakeout.

You will be looking for a dependable cash flow with no great or immediate need for heavy capital spending such as might be required by technological advances.

Your projected cash flow should be sufficient to provide reserves for receivables, inventory, and accounts payable.

You will now begin to qualify your proposed insider buyout for some of the rules of thumb of acquisition financing, although we won't get into the specifics of lenders and terms.

You will want an equity position of at least 51 percent and as close to 100 percent as possible to maximize your control.

Ideally, you will be looking for a comfortable assets-to-liabilities ratio of 2 to 1 or higher.

You will be looking for an annual yield on your equity of close to 100 percent counting appreciation, depreciation, and owner's salary and benefits.

Contingency Plans

Qualifying your division for an insider buyout also means adding an element of contingency planning to your visionary buyout ideas. Allowances must be made for the unforeseen and the unexpected. Your vision and insider buyout plans need to be realistic enough to allow for some worst-case scenarios.

You have developed contingency plans for your division as a part of the corporate hierarchy. Similar plans must now be developed for your division as a stand-alone company.

What if inflation and lending rates increase? What if they decrease? What would be your range of flexibility? What are the points that would trigger implementation of your contingency plans?

What if new government regulations change the way your products may be manufactured, transported, or sold?

What if technology makes obsolete a large portion of the way your division is doing business?

What if some of your key division assistants decide not to remain with the division after its divestiture?

What if some of the division's major customers desert the company after a divestiture?

Most important in this review of the qualifications of your proposed deal is the perspective of the seller. Why do you think the corporation may decide to divest your division? What's in it for them? Although an insider buyout may be your dream, will it solve problems and make people happy at headquarters?

"Making the decision to sell a business is probably the most difficult part of the divestiture process for a corporation." Leslie Frecon, the General Mills acquisitions manager said. [3]

Frecon said the most commonly named reason for divestiture is "lack of fit." Corporations also look to divestitures for improvements in the net economic value. She said they are most worried about the adverse impacts divestitures have on public relations.

"It may take management anywhere from months to several years to thoroughly examine and discuss all the implications of these questions," Frecon said.

"A divestiture is not without a certain amount of controversy, and it takes time to sort out the various internal points of view which may have developed over an operation's history....

"Management buyouts can be a viable option when the corporate seller knows and can trust management to be realistic, competent, and enthusiastic in their commitment to owning the business....

"Management has a tremendous advantage relating to their complete access to information about the business being offered for sale. To the extent that they can bring together the necessary constituencies in a discrete and professional manner, without affecting their ongoing responsibilities as managers of the operation, they can be competitive and desirable buyers," Frecon said.

If your insider buyout idea meets acquisition rules-of-thumb and still seems to you to be qualified from both inside and outside perspectives, you're still on track but it is time for some second opinions.

Vision, feasibility, and opportunity aside, can you make any money in an insider buyout?

Involving Your Counselors

This is a time when you're envisioning a major change in your life and fortunes and wondering, "How close to the ideal could this be?"

You believe that both you and your division have qualified as candidates for an insider buyout. But are you able to articulate that vision to others?

Now is the time to begin general discussions about your insider buyout ideas with one or two or, at most, three personal business counselors. Your purpose is to describe to them your vision of the opportunities that exist.

You are not looking for a confidant to tell you, "Go for it! Here's how to do it." That would carry more responsibility than most prudent advisors or counselors will want to carry.

Nor does your vision of an insider buyout want to wind up as an investment opportunity for some outside partner who wants to own and control a piece of your career.

But you will want the intimate involvement from your closest business counselors as your draft plans begin to mature into working documents.

Thinking, planning, and talking confidentially and separately with a couple of your counselors about a buyout of your division is not an escape. There are hazards in the insider buyout and tensions in these confidential discussions. You are not running from problems on this one. You are creating a whole different set of problems along with a whole set of new opportunities.

Be prepared for some fairly basic questions from your best counselors. Why do you want to take the risk? Do you know what it's like to run your own business? Are you aware of what it might require of your family? Is there enough time left? Are you too old?

As an insider, it is essential that you seek and find selected, skilled, professional, outside counselors.

But all you are sharing with your counselors at this moment is your vision. It is too soon to be specific about the dates, times, numbers, and personalities that you expect will characterize your insider buyout.

When the time comes, you will want to be able to tell headquarters honestly, "I have been looking at our alternatives for the division. One of the alternatives is selling it to management, to me. I have not run the numbers, but I have a feeling they would balance. Are you interested? Shall I come back with some specifics?"

Wait to hold your first detailed discussions about a proposed insider buyout, not with outsiders, but with company officials, with other insiders.

Chapter V References:

[1] "Born-Again Steel," by Craig R. Waters, *Inc.,* November 1984.

[2] "How's Your Vision," by Patricia Passmore McKeon, Vermont Consulting Group, *Chittenden Business/Vermont Business World,* November 1984.

[3] "Corporate Divestiture: The Seller's Viewpoint," by Leslie M. Frecon, *The Journal of Buyouts & Acquisitions,* August 1983.

Chapter VI

Planting the Seed

When you, the suitor, want to get married, you begin by sharing your vision of a happy life in the future. Then, when the time is right, you pop the question.

Similarly, for this insider buyout business marriage to happen, you, the suitor, must make the first move. You need to share your vision.

At this point in your consideration of alternatives, both you and the division are qualified candidates for an insider buyout. The division is a non-fit in the corporate family, and you can and are willing to support it on your own.

In our own case, the strategic planning exercise that Garden Way, Inc. had just started was beginning to clarify the essential function of that company. It was manufacturing and marketing. It was becoming increasingly clear to everyone that publishing was not going to be a central part of the future growth of Garden Way, Inc.

As in any courtship, this is a time of excitement, dreams, promises — and risks to all your longstanding relationships.

You are looking for a new, long-term relationship with the parent corporation. You are viewed as a trusted employee but now — surprise — you want to become an in-law. You have fallen in love with one of the boss's dependents, which you propose to make your own.

Your proposal promises to relieve your employer of worrisome responsibilities while at the same time making life better for the dependent.

This is no spur-of-the-moment elopement you are proposing. This will be a formal wedding, and at some point you will need to identify a best man and some ushers, those intimates who are going to stand up for you at this business wedding.

Impact On Your Life

An insider buyout is more than a career change. An IBO will inject itself more than a new job would into your private life, personal investments, and business career. Your business counselors should explore the impact of an insider buyout on your personal life from every perspective.

While you are preoccupied with your vision of solving business problems and finding personal fulfillment, your counselors should carefully consider the more mundane aspects of your business transactions. Your counselors will want you to come out of your deal feeling better about yourself, but not at the expense of your financial security.

You also need to educate your counselors about the environment of the corporation, in preparation for their dealings on your behalf with your corporate colleagues. Teamwork has been essential in your management of the division, and you need now to shape a team for help during your buyout negotiations and transition.

However, it is neither necessary nor desirable now to go beyond the generalities into numbers or other specifics with your lawyer, banker, or accountant. These details are best left until your vision has more than a speculative reason for existing. This is an insider buyout, not a takeover.

The primary role of your business counselors at this stage is to prepare you for hazards and traps you might confront in your role change from employee to entrepreneur.

This process of preparing to make an offer at the right time may last from a few months to years. In my own case, it took about six months. Others we spoke with waited patiently for up to two years. But many business buyouts have been consummated in as little as four to six weeks.

Your counselors should understand your perception of your

situation now so that they can have plenty of time to analyze and critique it with you in advance, all in preparation for their work during negotiations and transition.

You want them to be thinking about ways to effect a friendly, win-win deal. You want them to support a deal that makes the best of the situation on behalf of both parties.

In a successful insider buyout, the joys of the union far outweigh the tears of the separation.

It will be up to your counselors — your candidates for an acquisition team — to enable you to see the issues, comprehend the analysis, prepare for the consequences, and get you ready to make your move. But it will be up to you to create the vision of success and establish the goals.

Act, Don't Worry

"Don't spend years of anxiety" wondering and worrying about an insider buyout, advises John Jordan of the Jordan Company.

"The idea of approaching the parent company about buying out a subsidiary is a commonplace practice these days. That's one of the alternatives to think and talk about," Jordan said.

An insider buyout begins, he went on, when "a guy has something in mind. He talks to his friends. He starts generating ideas. And in most cases he comes up with the right combination. It's no different than the way the rest of the business world works. Start talking to somebody to see if you've got a viable idea."

Several of those we talked with agreed that the most successful insider buyouts are those that result from asking one question: "How do we work our way out of this corporate problem?" The process then determines that the insider buyout is the best alternative.

From a division manager's point of view, you've got to see the opportunity and it's got to be there. And the timing has to be right.

Tom Begel of Pullman Transportation carried this thought one step further in describing his buyout from The Signal Companies.

"You've got to be the initiator. You've got to develop the plan, find the dollars, and plan the structure. You've got to think that through, then say, 'Here's my plan to do it.'

"We first formed Pullman Transportation in 1982 in preparation to do something. We simply set up a separate company. That was in preparation for what nobody was sure. But it got the Pullman Transportation freight car business off the books and into a separate company.

"The official spinout occurred on February 24, 1984. It was nearly two years from planning through ultimate execution. Invariably it takes a whole lot longer than you would ever anticipate."

Profiling the Players

You must find the key person in the corporation who will make your vision of your insider buyout come alive at the highest levels at headquarters.

It is time for you and your counselors to meet at length to discuss in depth the business and psychological perspectives of each of your potential sponsors in the corporation.

This is called profiling the players.

You will want to profile them three ways: as individuals acting alone, as individuals acting within a corporate group, and collectively as a dynamic corporate group.

When your counselors are thoroughly briefed about the corporate culture and personalities, they will be able to help you identify your prospective sponsor or sponsors and those who might oppose the buyout.

Additionally, making your counselors familiar with the corporate picture will help them during negotiations. At all costs, at that time they must avoid doing anything that doesn't fit with the established climate of mutual trust, friendliness, and respect you share with your corporate colleagues.

Profiling corporate players is similar to evaluating politicians during an election campaign. Responsible news commentators and columnists don't collect gossip and speculation about the private lives of the candidates. They evaluate the relationships between people and organizations in qualitative terms. And so should you, in doing your profiles.

This profiling requires sensitivity to how power, data, and influence move within headquarters and between headquarters and the division.

This is no different from evaluating the personnel you hire or the suppliers you use. You ask, "Who's the most reliable? Who's the best producer? What's their track racord? Who will fit the best in this situation?"

Get Help

Because profiling involves assessing the relationships between people, and because no two persons are likely to understand the same relationship the same way, it is essential that profiling not be attempted alone.

For safety's sake in something as important as your insider buyout, seek opinions from among your closest counselors about the corporate relationships.

In most cases, your outside counselors will not know your corporate associates personally. But you will sit with your counselors at length while they take notes, ask questions, and develop a shared background of the business behavior, authority, and responsibilities of all the corporate officials.

This detailed profiling will include anyone you and your counselors may have to deal with.

One of the most important players you must profile is someone you all know: you. It will be of comfort and of inestimable value to you at this point if you are able to share your innermost thoughts with and accept objective criticism from your counselors.

In evaluating yourself and the others, consider background, ambitions, skills, interests, leadership styles — anything that might affect business relationships and behavior in negotiations for an insider buyout.

Who are the decision-makers as opposed to the title-holders? Who are the key decision-makers?

Whom can you trust? Who would serve as your sponsor?

You try to determine whose career would be helped if your insider buyout were successful.

Also, you try to determine who might be threatened by an insider buyout.

Look for corporation officials who might have a sentimental or protective association with your division. They might include one of your predecessors, a member of the original acquisition team, or perhaps the company founder.

Look for unusual corporate or personal interests that might need to be protected in your buyout try. This might involve longstanding employees or valued customers with discontinued products that need parts and service.

You are not seeking to separate white hats from black hats. You are seeking to share with your counselors the atmosphere in which your proposal will be received.

You are looking, too, for someone who will champion your insider buyout within the corporation, someone you can trust to act as your sponsor.

You ask yourself and your counselors, "Who has the most interest in seeing this corporate problem solved?"

Could Be Your Boss

This could be your boss or another superior. It could be a trusted headquarters-level adviser such as the corporation counsel or a member of the board of directors. It could be a colleague of equal rank. It will not be a subordinate.

It could be the corporation's chief executive officer. But soliciting support directly from that office may circumvent some key people whose support you will need during negotiations.

It could be the chief financial officer who wants a clinical solution to a cash flow problem. But this officer might not be effective as a project sponsor.

It could be your trusted in-house mentor. But it is more likely to be someone with whom you have not previously been close.

It could be an outside member of the board of directors. But such a person will probably not be effective at organizing support within the hierarchy.

You should take several months to consider and reconsider the players with your counselors. The questions about them are too important to try to answer alone or to discuss hurriedly with casual advisors.

Correctly identifying your best prospective sponsor may be the most important decision you must make in planning the insider buyout.

Raising The Question

As an insider buyout prospect you have optimism, vision, and a sense of the best-case scenario. But how will you articulate your vision of an insider buyout as a convincing reality to skeptical corporate colleagues?

You are approaching your key moment of opportunity in an insider buyout: the time to pop the question.

Your approach to headquarters is critical. This is your time of greatest risk. One misstep and you and your corporate confidants or sponsors could be fired.

You will be judged less on what you are doing than what you appear to be doing.

Be Cautious

Words of caution to managers about what they appear to be doing were recently given by buyout veterans Carl Ferenbach and Harold S. Geneen.

Ferenbach, formerly head of mergers and acquisitions at Merrill Lynch, is now a partner with the Boston-based Thomas H. Lee Company. [1]

Ferenbach said when a member of management suggests buying a piece of the corporation, the parent corporation's first consideration is whether to sell the division or replace the managers.

The next decision, Ferenbach said, is whether to sell the division to the managers who made the offer or seek other bidders. If they decide to seek other offers, then a further decision is needed: whether to allow the bidding managers to continue bidding in competition with the outside offers.

Geneen was a party to the insider buyout of TICOR, which we'll explore more fully in the next chapter. One of his remarks is pertinent for managers who are considering a little politicking at headquarters to line up support for an insider buyout.

"To insure open and honest communications it seemed to me that office politicking could not be tolerated. I announced this in unmistakable terms: if anyone tried to line up other managers to back his pet project in return for a quid pro quo later, or if anyone tried to force a man junior to him to give anything other than his honest opinions, he did so in peril of losing his job." [2]

Don't Give Wrong Impression

If you are careless in your first approach to headquarters, you could be interpreted as saying, "I know what's the matter with this division: you control it. If I owned it, I would make money from it."

Better to suggest: "We have a joint problem and we both need a creative solution."

This is the beginning of a whole new business relationship between you and your employer. Neither one of you will be able to think of the other again in the same way.

This is no time to play office politics, but it is a time to be political in the sense of being straightforward, yet diplomatic and fully understanding of office politics.

You were being diplomatically political in a thoughtful and non-threatening way when you profiled the corporate players.

You have identified the highly placed corporate official who has the most to gain and the least to lose if your insider buyout succeeds.

You have further qualified this key decision-maker as someone you can trust who will willingly help influence the other key decision-makers on your behalf.

Now you need to know how you can most effectively reach that person.

You are in a delicate spot. You are a part of the corporate team, one of the horses pulling the same wagon. You have business, legal, and personal relationships with the corporation, its owners, officers, employees, customers, and suppliers. Those relationships have created legal, ethical, and moral responsibilities that must be fulfilled.

Don't Wait

You do not need to wait for headquarters to drop the first shoe about selling the division. You have been participating in the process of deciding what is to be done with your division. Maybe your boss said it might be sold some day. Maybe the idea surfaced at a planning meeting. Maybe you suggested the alternative yourself in an earlier report.

You might be inclined to let someone else be the first to suggest an insider buyout so that you do not appear to be overanxious or greedy. If someone else suggests it, you might be further inclined to be coy and play hard to get.

But you could miss your once-in-a-lifetime opportunity if you delay too long or become too political about withholding your insider buyout idea.

You will want to be straightforward with your insider buyout vision, neither too aggressive nor too reluctant. By all means do not delay once you have decided: the corporation's chairman at this moment might be talking with an outside suitor.

A Possible Approach

You have selected a prospective sponsor who you expect will champion your vision of an insider buyout.

You plant your seed with this person carefully but informally over a cup of coffee or perhaps during a casual breakfast meeting.

"I've been struggling with my division. It's an odd duck. It isn't doing as well as it should. You know the numbers. We're stuck with certain overhead.

"I'm trying to find the answer for both the corporation and the division.

"In working through this, something struck me and I want to bounce it off you to see if it makes sense.

"We could sell the division to an outside company, or we could liquidate. But there may be an in-between situation that might be a better overall answer financially and from a public relations point of view.

"What if it were sold to management, to me, or to a group of us who would put up a stake and come up with a plan to maintain the accounts and save as many jobs as possible?

"Selling it to management could be quick and would save the company from bringing in outsiders.

"My job is to run through the alternatives and solve the problems. This appears to be one of a number of alternatives. I will think more about this option if there is any interest."

If you've picked the right person, your proposal will be well planted and will grow.

If you were mistaken and dropped your little seed on barren ground, there is probably nothing lost and you can reevaluate your sponsor prospects and try again. And again and again, if necessary.

But restrict your seed planting to chats during informal business situations. You are merely testing an idea by asking a few loaded questions.

Do not add the insider buyout item to a business meeting agenda and show up with a business plan.

The task here is to plant the seed of an insider buyout without upsetting the established corporate relationships and without giving even the appearance of a breach of trust.

You don't want to rush out and buy an engagement ring until you have some good indications it will be accepted.

At Garden Way

Just prior to our insider buyout of Garden Way Publishing, we had been through a particularly difficult period. Our results were short of corporate expectations. Generally, our division was not meeting standards.

Headquarters was saying, "We're never going to make any money in this. What are we in this business for, anyway?"

The first seed of our insider buyout was planted near the end of 1982 one evening over dinner with a member of the executive committee who had been reviewing our operations.

He said, "Why don't we get out of this? Forget about it. We're wasting our time. Let's concentrate on our winners."

I said, "If the company ever wants to get out of the business, I'd love to run it. Maybe there is some imaginative way we can do it."

This was over a good steak dinner. It was very natural, very easy, and almost mellow. We had no further discussion at that point.

The risk is low in this kind of seed-planting. This is not a confrontational situation. It is merely a clear expression of intense interest in a hypothetical situation.

I hadn't planned to go into the dinner that particular night and plant the seed of the insider buyout. The opportunity just happened. So much of corporate life is seizing the opportunity when the time is right.

I guessed at that time that the chances of our completing an insider buyout were only about one in three. But that was enough for me to begin spending time in some very specific thinking and planning about the possibility.

My friend from the executive committee did not mention the subject again until three months later at a breakfast in early March 1983. He said, "Remember that dinner we had up in Burlington? I've been thinking about that a little more. Do you really think that would make any sense?"

By this time we had a draft proposal with a lot of information, philosophy, and proposed legal structure — everything except the financials. We were ready to deliver a first "what if" memo within twenty-four hours.

Many Prospective Buyers

Dick Hug, who bought out Environmental Elements from Koppers in 1983, recalled his frantic days during the late summer and fall of 1982: "When the edict came from the board [to shed some units for cash to reduce borrowing], it was obvious that our company, which was out of the main stream of Kopper's core business, was an eligible candidate.

"I worked very closely with their business counselor at First Boston trying to identify companies that might be able to purchase Environmental Elements.

"With my help, Koppers contacted some potential buyers. A couple of candidates began vying for the purchase. These were other firms in the pollution control business that wanted to expand their scope."

Koppers sold a remotely related portion of Environmental Elements in Texas, which Hug said, "allowed me to get my arms around the balance of the business [in Baltimore], a chunk I felt we could handle.

"I made my mind up one Friday evening in late October when my wife and I were having dinner at Howard Johnson's. I got together with my financial guys on Saturday and Sunday. Then I hopped a train to New York on Monday to see if I could find some money."

He found an investment banker willing to back his insider buyout. While completing arrangements, he called from New York to arrange for a meeting that night with his boss, a senior manager of Koppers who reported directly to the chairman.

Hug's train from New York back to Baltimore was late, causing his boss to wait several hours.

"Our initial meeting was about one in the morning at one of Baltimore's better bars. I had a typed-up proposal.

"He had no idea what we were to meet about. He kidded me about being late. Then I handed him the envelope with my letter. He was somewhat amazed and said, 'You have been a busy man.'

"He took it to the chairman and deputy chairman who carried it to the board. Then I met again with my boss. All my meetings initially were directly with just him, just one-on-one.

"They took about three weeks to review the proposal. Later we had a handshake. They said, 'OK, we'll continue our negotiations with you.' And then we had a letter of intent that was signed in December, 1982.

"Once they accepted the proposal, they had a lot of due diligence they wanted to do, a lot of negotiating as regards to liability, and that took about six months to get ironed out."

Planned Early

Dick Snyder, who formed Snyder General Corporation from the heating and air conditioning division he bought from Singer Corporation, said, "when I joined Singer, I had in the back of my mind the idea of making an offer somewhere down the road.

"I sensed the timing was right, since Singer was going after aerospace and third-world consumer durables. I really didn't see a fit for the climate-control division. I went to my immediate supervisor and requested a meeting with the chairman and the president.

"Most large corporations don't truly understand LBOs. It's too easy for them to say 'no' to an employee. I felt I needed to be able to demonstrate that I could do the deal. I was concerned that they would summarily dismiss me if I went in there and said, 'Hey, I would like to go out and see if I could arrange some financing.'

"So I had letters of commitment with me when I first approached Singer. I had already arranged my financing, and I knew it was a do-able deal. I felt it could be done, and all I needed was the blessing of the chairman. That's the best way to do it, in my opinion.

"The Singer people were professional in every respect. They respected my business capabilities and what I was doing for the Singer Company. I think they respected the way I approached them, and it was done on a very professional basis by both parties. They may have had some conversations on their own that someone was irritated, but it was never transmitted back to me.

"If I had been dealing in a very volatile type of an organization, I could have been fired that day.

"I knew there were some risks, but I felt that the worst thing that could happen would be that I would go out and work for somebody else. I was prepared to take that risk. And I think I was at the right age, forty-three, so I felt that I was still very marketable if I had to go out and find another job.

"I first approached them in the middle of July of 1981 with a firm offer at that first meeting. That offer was eventually increased by about ten percent.

"They responded that they would consider the offer about ninety days later in late September. I'll bet I had indigestion every day for those three months.

Surprised the Directors

Bob Hagans introduced the subject of his insider buyout of Unitog by surprise at a board of directors' meeting in October 1983. Unitog was at that time a public company but a small, closely-knit family company with strong personal relationships among the family founders, management, and the directors.

"It did not make it easy for us," Hagans said of the surprise factor. "We had to do our planning and shopping for financing in total secrecy."

In a public company, an offer for outstanding shares will be futile if the financing is not arranged in advance because the only advantage insiders have at that point is speed in a race with hostile and wealthier outside takeover artists.

The Unitog board, which consisted mostly of long-time, loyal company supporters, was understandably annoyed at the secrecy and element of surprise.

Hagans said the directors were concerned about management's ability to pull off the deal. Their overriding concern was protection of the shareholders' interests, especially those of the widow of the company's founder.

"Once we made the commitment, we risked everything," Hagans said.

Dealing As an Insider

Once you share your idea of an insider buyout with headquarters, headquarters will quickly perceive that you are spending less time on the corporation's business and more time on your alternative careers and business opportunities.

However, if headquarters truly views the division as a problem and you as a trusted and competent manager, the officials will probably applaud your initiative and decide to do business with you.

Meanwhile, you are communicating daily with the corporation's key decision-makers. You began doing that when you broached the idea of a takeover.

You want to keep your insider buyout idea moving without exhibiting any anxiety or compromising your reputation.

You will most likely be called to a meeting shortly with the CEO, your sponsor, and others.

This is their meeting with their agenda, but you have an important objective of your own: you want to be viewed in a new light, as a buyout candidate. Achieve this image with a straightforward listing of alternatives. Maintain a serious spirit of cooperation. And exude confidence about buying and managing the division.

This is a meeting of dynamics and sensitivity. You bring two assets to that table — your vision and your reputation. If you're perceived as disloyal to the corporation or incapable of handling the deal, the deal is dead in the water. But if you have done your homework, it will survive.

Their Idea, Not Yours

Proceed into the talks as if it was their idea for you to list all the alternatives and report on them.

"This is my job: to bring you the bad news along with the good. My focus has been on this division, but I have been brainstorming with my staff and picking up ideas from listening to the rest of you about our problems. I think we've turned over every stone.

"A management buyout appears to be one possibility for solving problems for both the corporation and the division.

"It's an intriguing idea, but I haven't run the numbers and will not unless you see it as a mutual opportunity.

"Is this one of the alternatives you want me to consider? If not, let's bury it right now."

When pressed for more information, center your whole conversation around, first, solving problems of the overall corporation and, second, problems of the division.

Put the conflict of interest problem right out on the middle of the table and ask their guidance on the issue. It is better from your position as an insider that they ask for the numbers than for you to pull out a report you have been working on for months with outside counselors.

Assure them that in the meantime you are continuing to follow previously set corporation and division goals.

In short, behave the same way you would if you were talking about your job and future with the firm: friendly, loyal, enthusiastic, confidential, responsive, and mutually opportunistic.

Your whole pitch has been to the problems of the corporation. Remind them that a decision to get rid of the division may be an opportunity to review the company's overall strengths and weaknesses in a major restructuring.

If you have presented all of this properly, headquarters will appreciate that an insider buyout is an efficient technique for correcting an acquisition or diversification mistake without going public and inviting outsiders in for an inspection.

The corporate leaders will appreciate the liquidity and lessened responsibility that a buyout offers. And they will see the advantage of dumping the full responsibility for the ailing division on one or more trusted managers who will now pledge their personal assets and redouble their efforts to build the company and those assets.

You have been dreaming and thinking of an insider buyout for months. You could sit down and write a first draft of a business plan.

But now is the time to glance at your watch and get back to business at the division. When you get up to leave, leave your vision on the table at headquarters. Now it's their vision.

If they're thinking clearly, they'll thank you for it.

Quick Decision

As we described earlier, Larry Munini was notified in a meeting in Dr. An Wang's office that his software department was to be sold.

Upon leaving the meeting, he went out in the hallway, did a U-turn, and went back in and had a two-minute meeting alone with Dr. Wang. "I said I'd like to start a company and buy the product from him.

"My next step was to prepare a formal memo that confirmed my offer in writing to start a company and buy the product for $1.5 million.

"Another outfit came in to look over the merchandise. That company interviewed me and they wanted to know all about the product and sales to see if they should bid on it. To see if it worked. To see if it was for real. To see how much money it was bringing in. To see what the problems were.

"At that time I developed a confidant relationship with my immediate superior, a trusted friend of the Wangs. When I told him of my offer to buy the division, his eyes lit up and he said, 'Great, that's the greatest idea I've heard. I was going to suggest to you that you do it, Larry.'

"He said, 'How much did you bid?' When I told him he said, 'Naw, that's not going to cut it. You should have gone for about $3.5 million.'

"One or two weeks went by and $3.5 million became a talking point. Based on the competitive threat of this outside firm, I prepared a new letter to Dr. Wang confirming my new offer.

"Then we went into a stalemate mode. But I was given the status of being a serious contender.

"They had a meeting of all the employees of the department and got up and said, 'Guess what, we're going to sell this whole thing. But don't worry. Wang will take care of you. You'll all have jobs even if we sell the thing right out from under you. It's the Wang Way. Everybody will be transferred.'

"It's a benevolent place. They take care of people. They're very much concerned with making people feel comfortable and not job-threatened.

"At that time they said there were two bidders, an outside firm and me. That's when I got busy on the outside. They started formalizing things and I started getting busy, saying I better go out and line up some financing."

Others Were Looking

Tom Madsen was president of Key Electro Sonic (now Key Technology), a Milton-Freewater, Oregon, division of Applied Magnetics of Santa Barbara, when the division was put on the block in 1982.

"We were operating quite independently of Applied Magnetics. We had quarterly review meetings and monthly financial reports, much like you might have with a board of directors. As long as the financials were satisfactory, they pretty much left us alone.

"They had already divested themselves of all their other divisions, wanting to concentrate more on their main business of magnetic heads, which was growing very rapidly.

"As an employee of Applied Magnetics, I found myself hosting some groups through that were looking at Key as a possible acquisition. These were other companies that were either investment groups or in the food-machinery business.

"There's a certain selfishness involved in showing other groups through the operations when some are talking about retaining management and some are pretty clear they are not.

"Several of us at Key were already talking [about an insider buyout]. There were four managers involved at that time. We had a few informal get-togethers over a few beers, kicking ideas around and dreaming.

"And I had discussions with Harold Frank [Applied Magnetics' chairman]. I knew that there was still some long-term interest on his part in Key. I had known Harold for some years and he knew me well.

"Frank agreed to back the insider buyout and brought in a sixth partner, Edfred L. Shannon, Jr.

"We all felt the company had a lot of potential in terms of the products we had been dreaming of having for a couple years prior to that. So we didn't want to let go of that. We felt that a buyout was the best way to pursue those dreams rather than allowing the company to be sold to an outside group.

"We got together and worked out a reasonable relationship between the six of us and then presented our offer to Ben Newitt, my boss, the president of Applied Magnetics. Our discussions started quite informally in a meeting as individuals. We made it known that there was a group of us interested in some kind of a buyout. While they were looking at other potential buyers we wanted them to be aware that we would be looking to put a deal together on our own. It didn't come as a big surprise.

"After that, Harold Frank, as an independent investor, had no more dealings on the part of Applied Magnetics regarding the buyout of Key Electro Sonic. It would have been a conflict of interest. He stayed out of that deal and we dealt directly with Ben Newitt.

"There was caution on the part of Applied Magnetics to make sure it was handled as an arm's-length deal. They had sold other companies to people who were managers, and I think their experience had been fairly good with those companies. In a situation where they might be willing to carry any loans, they probably felt it was a better risk if management was to be involved.

"In our particular situation, our deal is structured so that if we meet certain financial objectives then we manager-owners can take more equity as time goes along. It's an earn-your-way-in sort of thing.

"I personally think that's healthier for all parties." Madsen said.

Trust Is Essential

The key to an insider buyout, according to Vermont State Sen. Doug Baker, an innkeeper, is "having a good working relationship with trust between you and the previous owner.

"He's not going to give you an opportunity to buy him out by holding paper if he doesn't trust you. He's got to be fully satisfied that you can manage the business, pay your bills, and keep your first and second mortgage payments up to date.

"He would probably rather sell it to somebody he knows will treat the business well than sell it to a stranger.

"He's got to know that you're going to manage this business....so that the business will grow....

"He's looking for someone to sell it to who has the energy and time to make it grow, to protect his investment."

Listening For the Other Shoe

Remember, this is friendly, fair, and productive.

Your no-fit, black sheep division is not earning the corporation money and meeting other corporation objectives.

You have suggested to headquarters that one possible way to solve this mutually embarrassing problem is to let you buy it.

This puts you into a strange, uncertain position until headquarters gets back to you with a strong affirmative signal to run some numbers on the idea.

While you wait to hear again from headquarters, your best positioning is to continue to be straightforward and up front in all your relationships.

Unless headquarters has put a lid on the subject, there is no reason for you to be coy or deny you have thought about a buyout.

There is even less reason to be caught promoting the idea.

You are hoping to enter negotiations with your employer for an insider buyout. One perceived breach of trust or duty on your part could result in not only the loss of that opportunity but also the loss of your job.

But you would also run the risk of losing your job by failing to solve the division's problems or by presiding over either a sell-off or liquidation. Your job has been on the line for some time and there is no need to worry about it now.

You are not asking for special favors. Your offer to buy out the division you manage is asking for less from the corporation than applying for a job there in the first place. During a job hunt, you are asking the corporation to do the investing and to trust that you will be able to manage. In an insider buyout, you are providing the money, management, and trust.

Nonetheless, you will need to avoid any appearance that you are exploiting a conflict of interest. There could be a lot of backlash about an insider ripoff, with speculation that someone is stealing something such as an idea, opportunity, trade secret, or customer list.

But there is no reason to be paranoid about your insider's role. You'll get some strange, sidelong looks from once-friendly colleagues in the corporate hallways, but the problem may be that they don't fully comprehend the situation. There is no predatory behavior on your part. You are not stealing. You have offered to help them turn lead into gold.

You are in a business setting, and fortunately you can expect most people to act according to customary business etiquette, which is to say they will mind their own business.

Shift in Relationships

But you will notice some shifts in your corporate relationships among those who are privy to your buyout suggestion.

Some will be relieved to think that something positive is being planned for the ailing division and it is not their shop that is being considered for a divestiture.

Others will be nearly gleeful, imagining the pullout of your division as a solution to some perceived threat or diversion of funds from their division.

Along the way you may also encounter jealousy, confusion, pettiness, or even competitiveness.

Take Harold Geneen's advice here and treat all these partisans similarily — at arm's length. Let the project live or die on its own merits as perceived by the owners, without trying to build a groundswell of support in the coffee shop.

Your positioning with the headquarters is still primarily that of a trusted division manager and only secondarily that of a volunteer for funding and managing a special project, namely an insider buyout.

Your assumption is that headquarters will soon move forward with your idea. You will help relieve it of a problem and it will help you buy something it now owns.

Get Action Plan Ready

You and your outside counselors must now have an action plan ready for a late afternoon phone call from the CEO giving you the go-ahead to present some numbers and a draft buyout plan.

This is still not the moment to usher in the team of lawyers and investment bankers from New York City. In fact, that moment will never come in this book about a friendly, win-win, insider buyout.

Instead, when you get that call, ask the chief, "May I ask for some help from Finance with those numbers? I'll send my assistant over with everything we have here."

You can get a lot of support from the corporation at this stage. This is a friendly deal, a mutual, self-help project. Everybody is still working together. You are going to share all your information. There is nothing hidden here.

The feasibility of your successfully financing the buyout soon becomes the focus of the corporation's interest. It wants to be sure that the buyout financing is assured before the deal is announced.

Ask for Help

It is also appropriate for you to ask the corporation's finance department for recommendations and introductions to bankers you might use.

Ask headquarters if you may use the corporation accountants for pro forma statements or if it would prefer that you retain an outside firm.

Ask if you may visit with the corporation's legal counsel to discuss the original acquisition or previous divestitures and what will be required of you and your counsel in your buyout. You are not giving away anything in these discussions or attempting to beat anyone out of professional fees. These are courtesy visits. It is nice to have a few moments with the corporation counsel or accountant before you have to show up on the other side of the table from them during formal negotiations.

If you must err at this delicate state, it is better to err on the side of appearing to be naive than to appear to be too quickly overmobilized with outside counsel.

Your continued apparent dependency on the corporation permits headquarters to retain its customary, paternalistic role towards you. This makes it comfortable for all the people there to help you own something they once cherished.

Gradually, it begins to seep into the corporate consciousness that if the deal can get speedily wrapped up in one tidy package, it will preclude your having to recruit help from the New York investment community which would require a lengthy evaluation by corporate assessors.

Headquarters has not only accepted your proposal now but wants everyone to hurry up and set the stage for an early wedding. This is business at its best.

Your long standing corporate-family membership will prove to be your major hidden asset in consummating this deal.

Chapter VI References:

[1] "L.B.O.s: A New Capital Market (And How To Cope With It)," by Carl Ferenbach, *Mergers & Acquisitions,* Fall 1983.

[2] *Managing,* by Harold S. Geneen and Allin Moscow Inc., published by Doubleday & Co., 1984.

Chapter VII

Structuring the Deal

The way you structure your deal affects the tenor of your negotiations, your future relationship with your current employer, and, most important, the shape of your future business.

You structure your deal focused upon your vision of your future stand-alone company.

Structuring your deal means determining the whole package of players, property, payments, rights, and timing. This is the pivotal point of your insider buyout.

The purchase price may not even be the most important ingredient.

Price Is Only One Ingredient

The purchase price of a business acquisition ordinarily is based upon earnings or book value. But in an insider buyout, the purchase price is only one ingredient in the recipe. Your deal needs to be structured to account for many other equally important variables.

You, the manager, know the company and your divison. You know the problems that must be solved, and you know your own abilities and goals. You are the one person best positioned to suggest the ideal components of your deal for both you and the company.

A well-structured deal will correct past mistakes and prevent future disasters.

A well-structured deal is the vehicle that will carry you from where you are to precisely where you want to go.

The well-structured deal — your deal — will solve problems for both you and your employer.

If your proposed deal does not address the problems of headquarters, you will certainly fail in your negotiations.

You must show that the expense and effort of selling to an insider are less risky, less divisive, and less disruptive than the process of selling to an outsider.

You know what you need from the deal. You aren't guessing the way a third-party buyer might. You have been aware of the company's operations for a long time. And your company, if it is anything like Garden Way, Inc., will tremendously appreciate the careful preparations that you've made. One of my colleagues at Garden Way said at one point, "This thing wouldn't be going nearly as smoothly if you guys hadn't done your homework."

You can ensure that your deal includes the components you need to make your insider buyout successful. You don't have to buy any forklifts to get the warehouse, and you don't have to buy the warehouse to get the inventory.

For example, the managers of the cable television business in Prince George's County, Maryland, that was owned by Storer Communications of Miami, bought the division from the Miami firm in 1983. But Storer didn't sell and walk away. The deal provided for continued capital spending by the parent company for the Maryland spinoff during the year following the buyout.

Another example: at the time Tom Begel spun off Pullman Transporation Company from The Signal Companies, the parent company had been providing the subsidiary with an account of $50 million for working capital. This account was cancelled at the time of the spin-out, but to ease the separation, Signal established a new account providing Pullman $15 million in revolving credit.

Successfully completing an insider buyout is not an intellectual exercise. It is an action-oriented business opportunity which can be detailed on paper, analyzed, and solved with common sense and everyday business judgment. You do not have to be a skilled deal-maker to create the best possible deal for an insider buyout. You hire the professional skills you need.

Every situation is different. It is vastly more important to understand all aspects of your own particular situation than to try to comprehend dozens or hundreds of other people's deals.

Negotiating Time Varies

For example, who is to say how long it will take to complete an insider buyout? Calvin L. Baird, Sr. bought back a company he founded, Metal Sales Manufacturing Corporation, from Gifford-Hill & Company in a $26 million deal that took only fourteen days to finance and complete.

By contrast, Tom Begel said structuring his $28 million Pullman spin-out began in 1982 and did not conclude until February 1984 — after a final "staggering....all-time-consuming" seven months spent writing the deal.

In most cases, the components of an insider buyout agreement will be founded on common sense, integrity, prudence, and a dash of imagination.

But an insider buyout does not lend itself to filling out forms in the back of a how-to-do-it-without-a-lawyer book.

A wealth of business and financial management publications discuss all aspects of buying and financing a business, but no one person could possibly keep up with the stream of new business books and magazines and newspaper articles that might pertain to your deal.

Help From Your Counselors

This is where the training and dedication to your deal by your professional counselors become absolutely necessary.

"A lot of benefits can accrue to you, but you've got to handle them properly. That's why you need a lawyer and a tax accountant right from the word go — to structure the deal right," Remington's Victor Kiam said.

It will be up to you to educate your counselors in all of the specifics and dynamics of your own deal as the situation develops.

And it will be up to your professional counselors to pore through the law library and call up the necessary computer references for the finer and latest points of law, accounting, and taxation.

As you proceed from seed-planting through detailed negotiations with your employers, you will want your most intimate counselors to be kept intensely and almost continuously involved.

However, you need to ensure that you alone control the essence and the vision of the deal. An insider buyout is a deal driven by a respected inside business manager. Not by an employer. Not by a lawyer. And certainly not by a lender or an investor.

Your counselors will help you write and execute your deal, but you are the insider and you must remain in control of managing and communicating your deal with your employers.

Defining the Terms

"The corporate seller looks for clean, simple transactions. This means [the] assumption [by the buyer] of all the assets and liabilities...." This according to Leslie M. Frecon, manager of acquisitions for General Mills, Inc. [1]

An even cleaner transaction would include only the assets and none of the parent company's debt.

Structure your proposed deal around everything you will need to be successful. Be prepared to ask for everything that you will need from headquarters.

But, as important, be certain your initial proposal includes everything headquarters needs to solve its most pressing problems, and offer it without making anyone ask.

However you decide, decide early. You need to know what goes in the deal, what stays out, and what chips you will put on the table before you go to the table.

The list of tangibles and intangibles that need to be considered and structured into any buyout deal is unique in each case.

You may be paying for buildings, equipment, inventory, and other assets, but the real fruits of your acquisition are what some business brokers call the four P's: people, products, profits, and potential.

Cash Is Key

Kiam summed it up differently: "Don't think profitability is the key. It isn't. Cash is the key.

"In a leveraged buyout or a management takeover, you're doing it with mirrors. You have a lot of debt load and you have to pay a lot of interest. And so it may mean you sell off inventory at a loss just to get the cash to keep yourself current on debt.

"The number one priority in most management takeovers or leveraged buyouts of small companies is to make sure you don't run out of money.

"It's the old expression: cash is king," Kiam said.

You may structure your buyout to include certain people in certain jobs, or you may shape the deal to cut the employment costs.

You may intend to add to the product line, or you may plan to sell off certain facilities and rights. It all depends upon your projected profits and future potential. And it needs to be well-considered by you and your counselors before committing to a deal with specific loan repayment requirements.

You need to decide about investors. Will this be a one-person buyout or will you be participating with other managers? Will management own 100 percent of the equity or will outside investors participate?

There is still no need to worry about the uncertainty of financing in the asset buyout of a private company. You have time, an insider's position, and your experience as manager of the target division on your side.

Chapter IX, "Financing the Deal," will continue the themes cited throughout this book. Do your homework. Build your team. Don't lose control. And don't get preoccupied with the financing. If it's a good deal with good management, the money is available.

Questions To Answer

Meanwhile, you need to decide about legal entities. You must decide who will be doing the buying and accepting responsibility for the loans.

Will you buy it in your own name? Or jointly with your spouse?

Or will you form a partnership? For tax and financing reasons, many of the most spectacular real estate and leveraged business buyouts are performed by partnerships.

Or do you need to form a new corporation to make the buyout? If so, what kind of corporation will it be? There are a host of choices available under state and federal tax laws that allow you and your counselors to attain your personal goals and that help your new business meet its needs.

Are there some assets in the deal that you should hold personally in an effort to shelter income you expect to realize, or to further other business purposes? These assets can be leased or licensed for use by your new business in a variety of ways.

Who will be the officers and directors of your new company? How will your control be exercised? To whom will you be accountable and in what manner? Will you volunteer to report to someone or will such reporting be mandatory? Can you live with the choices someone else might make? If you lose control of your financing you may lose your company.

Don't let these seemingly endless options or threatening possibilities intimidate you. You know what is needed to operate successfully, and personal control of your business life is the primary motivation in your effort. Don't let collateral issues like tax avoidance or financing considerations impede your effort to gain control and run your business well. You will be taking big risks here based upon your estimation of yourself and your business. Don't trade the success of your business for reduction of personal income taxes, and don't give up personal control for more capital than you need.

Consider the options carefully, but keep your eye on the ball. Consider both the risks and the real costs when you make these structural choices.

Points of the Proposal

Listed below are some of the many other broad categories of terms and components to consider while drafting an insider buyout proposal to present to headquarters:

Customers: What needs to be specified in the buyout about your future customer base? Will you retain exclusive rights to the customer list? Will you ask for a non-complete clause from your old bosses? Will the sellers be obligated to send you referrals misdirected to the parent company?

Personnel: What key employees are essential to the transaction? In the case of an asset buyout, will a labor contract be voided? What happens to employee insurance and pension plans? Are there employment contracts that headquarters will insist go with the buyout? Regardless of existing contracts, are there unwritten provisions for employees you hoped to change that headquarters will now insist be written into the deal?

Property: What real estate, equipment, and other fixed-life assets owned by the corporation are essential to the success of your proposed buyout?

Liquid Assets: Who will own the accounts receivable? What percentage of them is collectable? Who will own the inventory and how will its value be determined?

Other Assets: What are you willing to pay for the company or product name and trademark? What is the value of the goodwill? Work in progress?

Liabilities: When will you become responsible for accounts payable? How will timing of the deal affect accrued and prepaid expenses?

Taxes: After the sale what will the depreciable assets be worth to you as a tax shelter during the important early years of your ownership while you are amortizing short-term debt? How will the various transactions affect your personal income and taxes?

Financing: In a small, private business buyout, it is most likely you will want to pursue a deal free of existing corporate indebtedness. You will need assets as collateral to finance both the acquisition and working capital.

How much can you add onto your home mortgage? Do you have company stock you can swap? CDs you can put up for collateral? Relatives who will accept your note? How many of the payments can you expect to meet out of revenues? Is the company likely to finance any part of your deal? Will you need one or more partners from management? Or do you need a venture capitalist leading a group of major lending institutions into the deal?

Timing: Time is money, right? You may be in a better position than anyone else to stage a buyout, because you can act quickly. What is a natural time to effect the buyout considering tax years, market cycles, production, and vacation schedules?

Other considerations that must be dealt with in the structure of the proposed buyout include royalties, franchises, agreements with suppliers, service and parts contracts, product warranties, use of patents and copyrights, potential liability claims, insurance contracts, transfer of licenses and permits, and pension-plan funding.

There are also considerations that may not be written into the deal but need to be weighed along with the terms, because they will have an impact upon headquarters and ultimately affect your negotiations.

For example, selling a poorly producing division to management saves many public relations problems for headquarters if any layoffs are in the cards. On the other hand, headquarters will point with pride to your acquisition if after the buyout you act as a sub-contractor in continuing to serve some of their accounts.

Your vision of the buyout also needs to be considered while you write the terms. For example, will you institute a profit-sharing plan? It is best to keep factors like this plugged into your day-to-day review of projected finances and strategy as you continue to shape the structure of your buyout proposal.

The number of variables leads to an astronomical variety of ways the deal could be written. It is essential that you report all of your considerations to your counselors by way of developing a master checklist of your needs.

Begel said this is the time you need lawyers who will be unafraid to say, "You're crazy, it won't fit."

B.W. Moore, who bought out Geosource from Aetna in 1984 for $140 million, put it another way: "Retain the finest professional assistance available, regardless of the cost."[2]

While you are focusing on dynamics inside the corporation, you need counselors who can assess the broader consequences of various terms that are being discussed. In buyouts, financial, tax, legal, or accounting barriers may surpass the imagination or experience of local players and their counselors, but somewhere expertise is available for hire or sometimes for fun.

For example, TICOR President Bud Morrow calls the insider buyout of the Los Angeles title insurance company from Southern Pacific "a textbook case with a few wrinkles that Harold (Geneen) put into the deal."

Morrow gives credit for conceptualizing the $270 million buyout to Geneen, one of his three partners, and to Gerald Tsai, vice chairman of American Can Company, which took a major equity position in the deal.

Geneen "is a rare jewel," Morrow said. "We don't find too many of those."

Morrow said completing the TICOR buyout "took a remarkably long period....almost a year.

"It evolved a little bit as certain facts came to light. Values. Timing. But the basic outline of the deal was pretty much standard."

Morrow said his partners had informal understandings about the financing before the negotiations and rearranged the financing plans several times during the talks. But the final commitments were not concluded until seconds after the talks were concluded.

"Having someone as credible as Harold Geneen as the head of our team was of inestimable help. I don't think the other three of us would have had the stature to do it."

Morrow may be underestimating his own stature. He has participated in more than 150 acquisitions, many as the president of Avis when it was part of ITT.

What advice does Morrow have for managers planning an insider buyout?

"Call Harold Geneen. That's his business," Morrow said with the salty chuckle of a native New Englander, suggesting that you won't get any help from your friends unless you ask for it.

"I don't think we could have pulled it off without him.

"But first we had to give him the opportunity."

Presenting Your Proposal

Finally, the little seeds you planted have started to sprout. Headquarters invites you to present a specific insider buyout proposal.

Maybe you have been waiting for ninety days. Maybe you have been waiting for a year or more. Or maybe headquarters responded immediately to your suggestion of an insider buyout.

No matter how slow or quick headquarters is in responding to your suggestion for an insider buyout, plan ahead to ask for time to think it over if and when an invitation comes.

You do not want to appear overanxious or in fact be overanxious. Ask for a minimum of twenty-four hours to talk about it confidently with your family and sleep on it in the light of the latest circumstances.

Ask for sufficient time to prepare a draft outline of your Insider Buyout Proposal. The purpose here is to seize the initiative without appearing opportunistic.

A Planning Report

Your buyout proposal resembles a planning report, not a financial report. The proposal includes a few round numbers but does not attempt to set values or prices. It is more than a trial balloon, but it is less than an offer to buy.

The deal you propose must provide headquarters with solutions to problems that go way beyond your division.

This is a five or six page proposal which appears to be newly conceived and freshly drafted for the exclusive viewing by headquarters. It is a set of confidential recommendations from a division manager presented to superiors in a forty-five minute meeting. It is a proposal for solving corporate problems, not your how-to-get-rich plan. It is the brainstorm of a trusted manager, not a proposition from a New York investment banking house.

Your Insider Buyout Proposal is in effect an outline of your proposed buyout. It is a presentation of the proposed legal structure of the deal. It assumes you will be successful in securing financing.

In presenting your buyout proposal, choose a planning format that is comfortable and familiar but structured so that the company's major problems and concerns will be treated first and foremost.

Your presentation of your proposal to headquarters will proceed from problems to solutions and from concerns to safeguards. "This is the unfortunate situation at our division, but here is a way out. These are some concerns with that plan, but here is the insurance."

At every opportunity, from first mention to final handshake, begin and end your discussions with headquarters with reminders of why an insider buyout will solve corporation problems.

Listen intently to signals from headquarters that indicate its latest definitions of its problems. In the corporate setting, these often change rapidly. Your proposal should reflect current thinking.

Most important, listen carefully for its initial objections to your proposal, concerns you will need to address as you move into preparation of projected financial reports and the draft agreement to buy.

Running the Numbers

At some point in your initial presentation of a buyout proposal to headquarters, someone will ask you what you plan to use for money.

"The price on this deal, or any other deal, insider or outsider, is going to come from somebody's review of the books," you remind them.

Explain that the values will be best illustrated when current and pro forma financial statements are prepared.

"What are the inventory, the receivables, hard assets, current assets, work in progress, goodwill, all the factors?

"I've played with some rough numbers at home, but I have nothing that would satisfy our people in Finance.

"Is there enough interest at headquarters for me to pursue this idea by suggesting some values?" you ask.

Headquarters may still be lukewarm about an insider buyout. But it is certain to be ice cold to the idea of outside auditors poking around for those numbers on behalf of an outside buyer.

In the one management buyout, a firm of investment bankers caused a few eyebrows to be raised after it was invited by the board of directors to give a "fairness opinion" of management's offer. Not content to judge the fairness based on its own expertise as an investment banking firm, it went into the market in its role as a commissioned business broker and solicited bids from seventeen other entities it thought might have an interest in acquiring its client company.

This questionable activity in the name of a "fairness opinion" succeeded in handling all of the company's competitors inside information about it. But business ethics are alive and well. Many business leaders called the client company's president to report on the audacity of the investment banking firm.

In a smaller, private asset buyout where there is no need for auditors, you will be slowly moving at this point, step by step, toward the time when a preliminary decision is made by headquarters.

You are waiting for someone to say, "OK, why don't you go run the numbers on this deal? Then come back and we'll talk."

Headquarters will want to see how the proposed divestiture will affect its net equity, profit, and cash-flow. Additionally, it will want to see if your vision of a division as a stand-alone will have sufficient equity, profits, and cash flow to secure the necessary financing and bear the costs of carrying and amortizing the new debt.

More Facts To Present

Your next presentation to headquarters will include balance sheets and operating statements composed of information available from inside the company. If your division is not already organized as a stand-alone operating unit, you will need to construct a pro forma balance sheet based on your proposed outline of the buyout.

This is still not the moment in a friendly insider buyout to usher in your team. This is not negotiating or auditing. At this point, you are still insiders. This is a time for insiders to exchange information that outsiders would need an audit to find.

This is still a mutual self-help project. Everybody is still working together. You are going to share all of your divisional information with them, the good and the bad, the advantageous and the disadvantageous. There is nothing hidden here.

You can get a lot of support from the corporation at this stage. You aren't stealing anything, you are helping it solve a problem.

When headquarters asks you to run the numbers, you might ask it for a budget. "Do we need an accountant, or can Finance do it? I'd be happy with Finance, but would appreciate having it set up so no one thinks I'm on an end run," you tell the boss.

Your strategy here is twofold. This signals the beginning of research by headquarters into a possible buyout. It may already have the numbers it wants. This also serves as a reminder that you have waited for its signal before engaging outsiders to study confidential inside information.

In our own deal at Garden Way, Inc., we had tremendous help from the comptroller's office, a young "numbers cruncher" on call, a personal computer to produce spread sheets and alternative P&Ls. This was yet another "win-win" situation. It helped the company to understand the alternatives and helped us with the bank.

Remember, this is still your proposal, your project, and your division. You have opened a Pandora's box, but you can't let headquarters push you aside and take over.

Keeping Control

In the buyout of a large or public corporation, keeping control of the deal may be impossible. Singer Corporation brought in Goldman, Sachs & Co. to perform a "due diligence" study of Dick Snyder's buyout offer and survey the market for possible suitors. Snyder said Goldman, Sachs acted as the quarterback of the dealings for a couple of months while it conducted its fairness evaluation. This included writing a model business plan with the assistance of Snyder who had completed his plan six months earlier while shopping for financing.

Whatever the size of the deal, you, the manager, know the target division better than anyone else in the world. Remind headquarters you thought of the insider buyout proposal only after it asked you months ago to come back with a plan for solving the problems.

"You told me to fix it. At a planning roundtable last year, someone said I should consider selling it. I did. To me. Here's why it will work."

You stuck your toe in the water when you first suggested an insider buyout with headquarters officials. Those officials stick their toes in the water when they acknowledge that they are beginning to collect information.

Put another toe in the water now and ask the officials if they want you to consider a buyout to the extent of asking your personal accountant to run some numbers on your personal finances.

If you hear a "yes" here, it will be the third time. Yes, they will talk buyout proposal with you. Yes, they will begin to collect information needed to set a price. And yes, you should begin organizing a negotiating team.

This last step will give you the authority to begin carrying inside information to outside counselors.

At this point, headquarters will normally organize a divestiture team of representatives from finance, personnel, accounting, and other staff departments.

It might be appropriate now for you to take your accountant and the headquarters finance officer or divestiture team manager to lunch. Let them meet first in an informal situation where they can discuss what they will be looking for and how best to meet each other's professional needs.

At the same time, with an eye to the future, you or your outside counselors should begin preparing feasibility statements, pro forma financial reports, and ratio analyses with best- and worst-case scenarios.

This is not the time to begin educating your outside accountants and other counselors about your personal ambitions and visions.

You did that months ago.

No Misunderstandings

Let no misunderstandings develop now with anyone on your team of outside counselors. Keep them continuously provided with the latest version of your buyout proposal which outlines the structure of the buyout deal. Be certain that your account has not been delegated to a junior member of the firm for on-the-job training.

Ask your outside accountant to begin feeding you draft pro forma financial statements in preparation for the negotiating sessions which you hope will follow soon. Make it clear that all reports that are intended for sharing with headquarters must be prepared far enough in advance so that you will have time to edit and revise them. You will be looking for a way to present the numbers in a format that best illustrates the problem-solving possibilities of a buyout.

This is also a good time to ask your counselors to challenge your assumptions with some serious computer games of "what-if?" What if interest rates rise? What if they drop? What if the company delays selling for six months or a year? What if the plant has a fire? What if you lose your three biggest customers? What if there is an illness or injury in your family?

Maybe the number-crunching is too confusing and too important to turn over to outsiders.

Bob Hagans of Unitog has a background in finance and a hobby of running pro formas. These were valuable in planning for the management buyout during three weeks of intense early-morning and late-night strategy sessions.

"I doubt a hired firm could have come in and done it," Hagans said.

Whoever produces them, what you need are financial reports that will permit you to return to headquarters with a presentation of what the buyout proposal looks like with all the blanks filled in.

You might say, "This is what your book value would look like with the division out. Based on estimated fair market value, here is the book value of the division as a stand-alone. By contrast, based on projected earnings of 15 percent, here is the value of the divested division."

You show what happens to their building and what happens to your stock. You make logical assumptions about the inventory, the lease on the warehouse, the forklift trucks, the employee pension plan, and the payroll.

You are the only one in the world who could talk about your division in this way. You are also the only prospective buyer who would not be rushing to bring in outside auditors.

Agree on Values

Skip over discussions of sales price and proposed financing and begin agreeing on the values of such things as the leases and office equipment. Remain open-minded about the total values until all the numbers are on the table and everyone is talking and counting in the same language. If there has to be a disagreement, let it be over little and easily managed items.

These discussions over small numbers give you an early opportunity to stake out a claim on the things you need to make the divestiture a success and to refuse excess baggage that would drag you down.

Tell them, "If the divested division is to succeed at this level of financing, it would need to consolidate in one leased building and be rid of the warehouse, forklifts, and trucks. If the warehouse stays with the firm, you could find a tenant or take a capital gain and do the layoffs. If the warehouse goes with the buyout, we do the layoffs and take the capital gain, but the extra financing load of the property might kill the deal at birth."

This first look at the numbers is a dress rehearsal for negotiations. You are hashing over little pieces of the deal and watching for reactions. You note the numbers that seem to be accepted and the numbers where there is concern. You are not talking directly about price or terms, or debating any of the sticky points. This will come later in negotiations.

After focusing on the small numbers for awhile, someone may ask you again what you plan to use for money in your buyout.

You do not have to reveal your potential sources of financing. Sidestep the specifics you may have in mind. Assure them you will leave no stone unturned.

Will Company Help?

One of the stones to turn over — very carefully — is whether the parent company will help with the financing. But don't frighten them with any hints the deal hinges on their participation.

Another stone: leading a large group of managers into the deal.

At Universal Electric, eight managers bought the company from Gould for $45 million with only $250,000 in cash. They retained 25 percent equity with an average cash commitment of only $31,250.

At Purex, twenty-three managers avoided an Esmark takeover in 1982, taking the company private for $440 million with $3 million in cash. They retained 10 percent equity with an average commitment of $143,000 each. Twenty-one of the junior managers had an average commitment of only $107,000 each.

At Converse, thirty-seven managers bought the company from Allied in 1982 for $100 million with $8 million in cash. They retained 33 percent equity for an average commitment of $216,000. Most of the junior managers had an average commitment of only about $75,000.

However, don't agree to terms this early in the talks with anyone — investors, lenders, or sellers. You are not buying a business on a retail market. The seller does not get to set both the price and the terms.

You have been studying the financial data for months if not years. You are going into the deal loaded with management skills, experience, ideas, information, and time — if not money.

You take the position that when all is said and done, the deal will float or sink on its own merits.

Dealing as Insiders

Suddenly, while you are discussing the numbers with headquarters, you sense that the corporate loyalists are beginning to pull away from you as you increasingly become the champion of alternative corporate business styles and goals.

You're pregnant and there is no turning back. The division is for sale and it is now a matter of haggling over the terms.

This is another delicate time. Your inside lines of communication are beginning to evaporate and your own team of counselors needs to be ready to take its place around the table.

Now you are facing your old friends in the corporation and their interests, if not opposing, at least are different from your own interests.

For example, Larry Munini's buyout of the software business from Wang Laboratories was structured as a win-win-win deal which was good for Wang, good for Munini, and good for the software business.

Munini explained: "From the beginning the concern was, 'Who would be able to take the software package out of Wang and keep the customers happy so that Wang did not get a black eye?'

"My proposal was that I was going to recruit from the current staff. I know the product. I know the customers. They know us. They love us now and they'll know us and love us when we're on the outside.

"That was the part of my pitch that I felt was part of my competitive advantage.

"Our customers are the Fortune 1000 companies. Wang was making a major sales thrust to the Fortune 1000 companies. Wang people were very concerned that Wang did not get blamed for problems with the software spinoff. They didn't want to have one of their salesmen going in trying to sell a Wang computer and get blamed for software problems in involving their whole payroll operations.

"That was the strength of my proposal, why they should sell the department to us and settle for a whole lot less money than they were likely to get from another outfit.

"The assumption was that I was going to recruit from the current staff in the department. The problem there was that there were about seventy people in the department and I was going to take about twenty-five of them.

"So the internal friction began as people formed opinions about whether they wanted to go with me or stay with the big company.

The petty bickering started at that point."

Yes, jealousies and friction will be a part of every buyout, including even friendly, win-win insider buyouts.

Remember Your Role

However, you still remain dedicated to finding answers for corporate problems with the division — and way beyond the division. You enter preliminary negotiations continuing to think and act in terms of the corporation's needs.

It is your duty to be honest about every possibility you see for the division. Illustrate your vision to the point of budgeting for a five-year plan.

You run the danger of success within the corporation at this point. The plans and numbers you produce could lead it to have another look at the potential of the division — possibly with another manager who is less restless.

There's a need for balance here. Don't burn any bridges. Don't betray any trusts. But don't avoid asking for everything you need to be successful. You also need to negotiate in terms of your own needs.

At this point in the Garden Way Publishing buyout, we remained oriented towards the corporation and they were genuinely concerned for us. This was the point where they were trying to find a way for us to own something, something for which everybody perceived we had a great deal of affection. This was the opposite of a taking - out or a takeover.

However, you cannot guarantee headquarters will continue to treat you as one of the family once you have admitted to the idea of eloping with the division. Your leadership and communications skills for managing an operating division are different from the skills needed for methodically assembling and negotiating a business deal.

The success of your negotiations with your employers for an insider buyout — and the very survival of your future business — sinks or swims on the way you write the deal and conclude the deal.

When all of the numbers are in, your attorney or accountant can begin making observations: "Here's the price tag based on this level of sales and assets. Based on that, we could survive and might make this profit. But we need to find a way to get the following resources."

No Arguments

Whatever you do, do not let anyone on your team argue or even show amazement at the suggestion of a very high selling price. Regardless of how exorbitant the first numbers might sound, play it straight and courteously. If forced to comment, agree that the company's assets are of great value and you hope you will be able to afford them.

There is no point in scaring anyone at headquarters into believing that you only want the division if you can steal it.

Unlike negotiations in politics, war, and love, business negotiations involve objective measurements with very little clouding. It will be easy for the professional negotiators on your buyout team to reduce business differences to economic terms.

At this stage, you are well beyond notes and outlines and are dealing with spread-sheets and a draft agreement.

You need to be in almost daily contact with your lawyer as well as your accountant, telling them of issues that will need to be studied and negotiated later, and telling them of points that seem to have early acceptance and may be considered already structured into the business deal.

This time of informal talks surrounding the number-crunching is a priceless time of negotiations among insiders. In agreeing how the numbers will be presented you're setting the stage to negotiate the deal.

Making Your Offer

The odds of your quickly obtaining financing for the buyout soon become the focus of the corporation's interest. Like you, corporate officials are anxious to get on with their main mission. Further, they want to be sure that the buyout's financing is assured before word of the deal is leaked.

More to the point, if the deal can be concluded speedily, it will preclude your having to seek financing from distant investors or lenders who would send in an accounting firm to perform a long and costly "due diiigence" study.

Few interruptions are as disruptive and demoralizing to a firm's ordinary course of business as having outside auditors parading through its offices retrieving files, asking suspicious questions, and laboring over minor mathematical errors in a search for something wrong.

Your corporate-family membership is the key asset you have in this circumstance. You trust their numbers and they trust yours. You have prospered and grown with the firm and if your buyout project falls through, you would expect to be still employed. This is a friendly deal and both sides are still looking out for each other's interests.

The firm is not losing an employee. It is gaining a buyer, a mortgagee, and perhaps a sub-contractor.

Be Honest and Direct

It is critically important that you continue to be totally honest, direct, and empathetic with the corporation.

However, rosy relations between the buyers and the sellers do not always last. Richard Genth, who purchased the Chris-Craft boat division from the diversified Chris-Craft Industries, said, "I felt like I had just gotten out of prison.... We're not even talking anymore." [3]

Keep Counselors Informed

Continue to report in detail to your counselors about each meeting or conversation you have with officials at headquarters. Tell your advisers who said what, who said nothing, and who just rolled their eyes. Not only will this debriefing be useful for planning your negotiating strategy, but the sharing of details will serve as a vital pressure relief exercise.

Your business judgments will be challenged at every turn during this period by associates who are beset with their own personal concerns. Some of your friends will never agree the division should be divested. Others who have not been your friends will happily begin promoting the idea of your departure. The pressures will build as it becomes apparent that some of your old friends in the firm will suffer real or perceived losses in power — or perhaps a real loss of employment.

One of the attractions of our insider buyout to Garden Way, Inc. was that they knew that we would make every effort to preserve jobs. By contrast, a liquidation would mean more than sixty jobs lost, and a sell-out to an outside buyer left the question of continued employment up in the air.

But it will be of great comfort to have your own team of personal counselors guiding you away from personal or emotional considerations as the pressures build in your buyout negotiations, especially since your major hidden asset in consummating this deal is your longstanding corporate-family membership.

Finally word comes that officials at headquarters are seriously considering your proposal. Now they want everyone to hurry and set the stage to conclude quickly or change the subject and get back to work. You arrange for your attorney to meet with the corporate counsel to confirm your intentions of securing financing for the buyout and to begin planning for an early closing if price and terms can be negotiated.

You are asked to make a non-binding offer in a confidential letter of intent.

Chapter VII References:

[1] Leslie M. Frecon, *The Journal of Buyouts & Acquisitions,* August 1983.

[2] B.W. Moore, CEO, Moorco International Inc. (oil field development services), *Structuring and Financing Management Buyouts,* Buyout Publications, Inc., San Diego, 1984.

[3] "Going Private," by Craig R. Waters, *Inc.,* February 1983.

Chapter VIII

Negotiating the Buyout

You've been invited to submit a letter of intent.

And, of course, you have it ready, having anticipated the invitation. You submit it.

It's a good letter. It covers two basic points:

1. It sets the tone of the upcoming negotiations. It's friendly, optimistic. It expresses the goodwill the parties feel for each other, the dedication of both to structuring a deal that works to the advantage of both.

2. It outlines the deal in the broadest of terms. It does not attempt to spell out the details. That will come later, in the negotiations.

Your team of counselors is prepared, and they've prepared you, briefing you on the complexities of the deal, as each one sees them from his vantage point. With their guidance, you've drawn up your list of goals for negotiations, planned your strategy for the sessions.

You're sold on your team. You're sure they are professionals who can tackle the tough issues, mount strong defenses when they're needed. You've made sure they know the company representatives at the bargaining table — who they are, their corporate roles, their influence with the others, their strong and their weak points, the tiniest details about them.

You're ready to do your part to make the negotiations go smoothly and quickly. You remember the advice of Leslie M. Frecon, manager of acquisitions for General Mills: "Financing sources and legal and accounting expertise should be in place on both sides, so that the first draft of the contract can be prepared within a week." [1]

Summing up, you're ready for this big, important step, the step you've been preparing for in these last intensive weeks or months of work.

You're ready to negotiate.

Lower Risks Now

In reality, although the stakes may seem higher during negotiations, the risks may not be as great as they were in the initial stages of the buyout. Many of the important decisions have already been made.

Compared to the uncertainties of planting the seed and structuring an insider buyout, negotiating the deal, even though exhausting, can be fulfilling.

Both parties know each other well. It is unlikely that deal-killing, unrealistic demands will be presented during the final stages of negotiation. In most cases, the talks will proceed under control and according to schedule.

But the threat of collapse in the talks still exists. This is no time for complacency.

Negotiations for an insider buyout are not so much specific events as they are a process — a process likely to span a period of several months. You will need to be on your toes for the entire period.

Negotiating will include everything from formal talks between the parties and their attorneys to informal agreements among advisors over minor points.

In the end, the series of agreements on major and minor points will be renegotiated, written up, signed, and delivered into one final agreement.

At times, you will want and need professional negotiating help continuously at your side. At other times, all you will need is advice over the telephone. And at still other times, you will be negotiating by yourself according to your script.

Weighing Your Points

No matter how carefully you and your counselors plan your negotiations, invariably some of your assumptions will be wrong, and these will lead to changes in the outcome of negotiations on certain points. It is essential that you memorize which points are vital to your plan, which points are only desirable, and which points you can afford to give away.

In an insider buyout, you need to expect the unexpected and to know in advance whether you are going to put your foot down, pass, or stall on any point that might arise at an unexpected time. In short, you must be ready to negotiate on unique points during unannounced encounters with unfamiliar persons in unusual places at unnatural times.

For example, what would you say if you were walking down the corridor and were stopped unexpectedly by the chairman who said, "Our position has shifted. Can you get this wrapped up in a week?"

On one hand you want to be agreeable. But on the other hand the timing change may demolish your marketing or financing plans.

On questions such as this, you might say that you would like to turn it over to your team of counselors. But there may not be time. Further, to do so on almost every decision might mean that you were losing a grip on the negotiations, were failing to understand all of the issues. What pieces will go with the new company? Who has liability in certain instances? There will be dozens of questions like these that you must answer now, and that you must understand when, down the road, you are running your own company.

An insider buyout is a manager's deal, not a lawyer's deal. That means you need to remain attuned to your feel for the players and property. You do not want to become so distracted by the negotiating process that you forget the rules of thumb of your business experience.

Go as far as you can alone. Then be ready to admit to yourself and your counselors when you have reached the limit of your knowledge and need help with negotiations, contracts, regulations, and their ramifications.

Leave the points that threaten the deal for your professional negotiator.

How well you and your counselors work as a team in managing this strung-out, bit-by-bit agreement process will determine the success of your final negotiations, and ultimately the success of your business.

Maintaining the Momentum

Once you enter negotiations with headquarters, a lot of wheels are in gear. You have momentum on your side.

A deal builds momentum from the active energy of its participants. It becomes a business priority for headquarters to complete the deal and clear the schedule.

As manager of the deal, you will need to move with the momentum or risk becoming trapped in a bog of inertia.

Tactics of Timing

For a buyer, timing is more important in an insider buyout than in other types of acquisitions. In an insider buyout, the seller is apt to control the timing.

Headquarters will jump and bend to accommodate an outside bidder, but in an insider deal, you will be the one expected to do the accommodating. This could lead you into some costly, even risky, delays.

Think speed. Don't let it slow down. Schedule the talks when officials at headquarters are likely to be untroubled by other major concerns and pleased with your recent performance.

Moving With Speed

A classic example of managers moving with speed, precision, and effectiveness on an insider buyout is told by Arvida Chairman Charles Cobb, Jr. and President John W. Temple. Arvida is a large real-estate and resort-development company with interests in Florida, Georgia, and California.

Temple had just returned to Miami from Atlanta and was driving towards his Boca Raton home when his auto-phone rang.

It was his boss, Cobb, with some surprise news: "My God, they're selling the company. What are we going to do?"

At that time, October 18, 1983, Arvida was owned by Penn Central Corp. The conglomerate had offered shares to the public in March, but investors weren't buying.

Cobb had been notified of a Penn Central board meeting in New York the very next day, a meeting called to approve an offer from an outsider to buy out Arvida.

Cobb and Temple met that night at Arvida's Boca Raton head-quarters to pore over lists of friends and acquaintances who might invest in an insider buyout. On the list were the billionaire Bass brothers of Fort Worth, one of whom served with Cobb on the board of trustees of the Stanford University Business School Trust Fund.

An Arvida secretary made arrangements for a chartered plane, and Cobb and Temple met the Basses in a Fort Worth restaurant that same night.

"We discussed the deal over beer and chocolate soufflé," Temple told *Miami Herald* business writer Emilia Askari. [2]

By 2:30 A.M. the pair had finished detailing a deal with the Bass brothers and were on a jet to New York and the Penn Central board meeting.

Their initial offer to buy out Arvida was rejected by the Penn Central board. But so were the first offers of two other bidders. For nine days the bidding went on. Most of that time Cobb and Temple spent waiting outside the board room. Three times they raised their bid with the backing of their new Fort Worth partners. Back in Boca Raton, the other Arvida managers were putting in twenty-hour days providing them with long-distance support. Finally, management's bid — $181 million in cash — was accepted on October 27.

The key to their backing by the Basses, Cobb said, was, "John and I and the other executives put up a very high percentage — basically all — of our net worths.

"We figured we had less than a five percent chance of pulling it off...," Temple said, "but if the company was going to be for sale, we wanted to be the buyers."

Tactics for Communicating

The business press fosters a popular notion that the main reason investors do a buyout is to turn around in five years and make a killing taking it public.

This thought may never have crossed your mind. But you will want to follow religiously some administrative and communications practices, tactics, if you will, that will forestall such suspicions.

You were straightforward in proposing the buyout to headquarters. And you will want to be straightforward continuously with all the other functionaries and bystanders who ask you about the buyout.

This job was made easier for Larry Munini at Wang Laboratories when officials announced to employees that there were two bidders for the software department, one of them Munini, and that all employees in that department would be offered transfers, rather than being laid off.

From the very beginning of your buyout discussions, focus on the obvious reasons why you have the skills, experience, and career interests to run the company for the rest of your life.

Be trusting and trustworthy. At the same time, proceed independently in assembling your deal without appearing to be subservient to headquarters personnel.

Listen carefully and look hard to find areas of agreement.

Build your case through the personal relationships you have in the company. The mood of the talks should be "very adult, not emotional," said Bud Morrow of TICOR, who has participated in over 150 acquisitions.

Sharing Information

In our Garden Way Publishing deal, Garden Way, Inc. officials never felt we had any secrets up our sleeves. We were sharing information with management at every step. Their accountants and lawyers had the same information we had. There were never any substantive surprises.

Following straightforward administrative and communications practices from the very beginning will be particularly comforting to you if the buyout talks drag on for months while you are still running the division.

"These negotiating sessions are slogging contests," said Jerry Gura of CWT Specialty Stores. "They are very lengthy, especially in leveraged buyouts."

Gura's negotiations were strung out not only because of difficulties finding financing but also because new leases had to be arranged for each store throughout New England.

"That took us about a year and was very complicated but very successful," Gura said. "Our landlords were as excited as we were about our growth progress and what we were bringing to them in additional business."

After Dick Snyder made his insider buyout bid for the Singer Company's climate-control division in July, 1982, he had to wait three months for the other shoe to drop.

"Singer came back to me in late September," Snyder said. "That's when they said they would bring in Goldman, Sachs to be the deal coordinator and quarterback."

To ensure that Singer would receive the best price, Goldman, Sachs spent over two months performing a "due diligence" study for Singer and scouting other prospective buyers.

"There were one or two other prospects that led me to up my offer about ten percent," Snyder said.

It was December before Snyder and Singer completed the evaluations and entered a long period of negotiations.

"I still continued to operate the business, although they assigned a corporate finance officer to review all our transactions subsequent to our letter of intent. They wanted to protect themselves and avoid anything that I might do that would not be in the Singer Company's best interests."

Preparing for Sharing

Successful negotiations in an insider buyout are a process that is nine-tenths preparation. It is not something you can practice.

Most managers will have only one opportunity to do an insider buyout. Everyone we've talked to called it the thrill of a lifetime and a valuable education.

However, preparing for an insider buyout does not mean you need to become proficient in any unusual deal-making skills. An insider buyout is just another workable business deal that may be analyzed, priced, packaged, and closed without extraordinary intellectual involvement or prior experience.

Your role as a professional manager and driving force behind an insider buyout is to prepare for the talks by planning how to organize and control the financing, structuring, and negotiating.

You personally do not need to be educated or even skilled in negotiations, accounting, financing, taxation, or acquisitions. As a professional manager, you have retained professional counselors who provide know-how in these areas.

The expertise you bring to the table is that of the division manager. This is what the talks are all about: improving the management and solving the problems associated with the division.

The better prepared you are, the better you are going to negotiate. The better you have done your homework, researched and analyzed the issues, the more you have sought out professional advice on specific questions, the better negotiator you will be.

In our Garden Way, Inc. negotiations, we noticed that the better prepared we were going into our meetings, the better we seemed to come out of them. It wasn't so much learning magic negotiating skills as it was simple, hard preparation. And it can frequently smooth what could be rough spots. Our specific knowledge of the inventory and receivable situation, as well as authors' advances and work in process, all of which might have been complicating factors, just weren't because we knew them so well.

Your counselors will prepare for the negotiations with research into their areas of expertise. They will orient you on what to expect and give you recommendations on how to respond.

Keeping Control

Meanwhile, you will need to focus your preparations on retaining management control of the deal in a positive way.

There are at least two ways to ensure that you keep control:

1. Prepare for the negotiations with the attention to detail of a prudent manager. But do not let yourself become so transfixed by the mass of details that you forget your primary role in the talks is as a sales manager. Think of the talks as a prolonged and final sales presentation. Enter the talks with the imagination and enthusiasm of a winning salesperson.

2. Center your preparations around solving problems and finding agreement.

Looking for a Win-Win Deal

The deal you propose must provide headquarters with solutions to problems that go way beyond your division.

In any deal that is well structured, the parties will share the benefits as well as the risks. It's a matter of exploring what winning and losing mean to each party and then working to avoid a losing situation for either party by minimizing the downsides.

Lou Auletta of Bauer/Electro said, "I wasn't looking for a steal. And they weren't looking to make all kinds of big profits and take advantage of me. It was a very fair negotiation and turned out to be a very fair deal."

Larry Munini said his lawyer was invaluable in putting him at ease over assurances demanded by the Wang Laboratories attorneys and, at the same time, pointing out areas where he should ask for a better deal. The pair negotiated a fifty-page agreement for the buyout of the software division from Wang in only one day of working sessions.

"I knew that organization," Munini said. "I had been a manager in that organization for a long time. I knew how it would work. When I was on the other side of the table, there weren't any surprises for me. I knew what their motivations were.

"The only one who was surprised was my attorney. He said, 'I can't believe these guys. They let you recruit a staff. They are willing to let you take all these materials. This is unusual.'

"I said, 'Hey, I'm part of the deal. I'm going to make their customers happy so Wang doesn't get a bad reputation. That's part of their thinking.'

"I was in essence one of them. I knew their priorities and was positioning myself to take best advantage of this. That was my whole sales pitch. 'I know the customers. I know the product. I can do that for you.' I knew what their hot points were. That got us through the negotiations.

"I think that is definitely the advantage of being an insider in a buyout like that."

We certainly felt the same way at Garden Way, Inc. The name would continue to be used under the licensing agreement. Our books would, in effect, advertise the Garden Way, Inc. name. We *were* part of the deal.

Manager in Control

You will do better by informally outlining your deal directly with your employers before involving outside lawyers. Later, lawyers are vital to ensure that all potential threats are exposed and that all the expectations on both sides are shared and communicated. But don't let the lawyers become too busy too soon and escalate the anxieties.

Try to negotiate at all times from a flexible position.

If things get rough or bog down, be ready with some options that you can suggest.

Dick Snyder points out one disadvantage employed managers have in an insider buyout: "You don't really have the [negotiating] leverage [of an outsider]. There were some things, because I was an employee, they said, 'This way is the way it will have to be.'

"They had some things that were not negotiable. I could have made strike issues out of them. I could have said, 'Let's make it more arm's length. That ought to be a negotiable item.'

"There are some things in the contract that I probably would not have accepted if it had been completely arm's-length negotiations and I had not been an employee....I swallowed my pride a little from a business point of view and accepted some things with the objective of getting the company.

"But my position was, if the deal doesn't go through, what have I got? I'd still be somebody's hired employee. It's not as though you already had your own business or a half a dozen alternatives that you could buy. I had to get the keys."

Counting on Your Counselors

Don't bring your lawyer into the insider buyout talks until your employers first introduce theirs. And caution your attorney about avoiding any appearances of overkill in your buyout negotiations. Most lawyers are accustomed to performing as the quarterback on the deals they do while the parties sit on the sidelines and sign their names on cue.

Make it clear with your lawyer that the insiders will outline this deal. Make it clear from the beginning that this is a friendly insiders' deal, not a competition between rivals.

There should be very little of your lawyer's ego at stake in your deal. Professional pride and skills, yes. Ego, no.

Jay Jordan, the venture capitalist, best described the key strength that lawyers and other professional counselors bring to the deal: "Experience."

"Knowing. That's the key to success [in negotiations]," Jordan said. "The guy who hasn't been through it before is not going to know when to give, when not to give, what to say, and what not to say.

"An experienced person will know.... The experience may result in a non-transaction, and that might be good.

"Just because the division is for sale and there is a viable buyout candidate is no sign of a deal."

Completing the Profiles

In Chapter VI, discussing how to profile the players, we stressed the importance of making your counselors intimately familiar with the people they'll face across the bargaining table.

If this is done effectively, your team will have fewer surprises during negotiations. You and your counselors will know the other negotiators so well that their reactions to specific points of the deal will be predicted. You and your counselors should know which of the company negotiators can be expected to speak on such issues as accounts receivable, company vehicles, or pension plans — which will speak and what they will say.

Fine-tuning your profiles for your counselors is not something that is done once, then forgotten. In the period between the formation of your team and actual negotiations, you will be in contact with these company representatives in meetings and telephone conversations. Keep your counselors up to date on these contacts, no matter how trivial they may seem, so that your counselors' images of these company people mirror your own.

Similarly, when actual negotiations begin, you should meet with your counselors after each negotiating session and debrief each other. Which of your assumptions were correct? Which were off base, and because of this should your strategy be changed in any way? Were there any surprises? Who was offended? Why?

The dynamics within each corporate family are so different that you will be putting your counselors at a disadvantage and limiting their help to you if you do not take the time to profile carefully the players before and during your negotiations.

In the early stages of our Garden Way Publishing buyout, I was scheduled to meet with corporate officials for dinner and an evening meeting at a motor inn in Saratoga Springs, New York.

To be fully prepared for this key meeting, I met with Don the morning before and ran through all of the probable issues and the corporation's probable positions: if they say this, you say that; if they say that, you say this. I put it all on tape and listened to it in the car on the way to Saratoga from Williamstown.

The way the talks developed, it was almost as if both buyer and seller felt they had "written the script."

What's It Worth?

There is discipline in business negotiations. There's a way to win, a way to lose, and a way to keep score.

Compared to domestic, labor, political, or diplomatic negotiations, the differences between the parties in business negotiations are easily quantified and manipulated.

It is comparatively easy to reduce business conflicts, perspectives, goals, motives, or experience to economic terms.

In business negotiations there is a way of compensating for loss and providing opportunity for gain.

One way to help keep the negotiations friendly in your insider buyout is to look upon the process as an information exchange, a time for everybody to exchange reasons for setting values.

In arm's-length negotiations among outsiders, the parties may frequently become arbitrary about their values.

In insider negotiations, the parties have been continuously sharing values and the adoption of an arbitrary position would be foolish, if not fatal, to the deal.

Nonetheless, it is best to appear open-minded about the values until all the numbers are on the table and everyone is talking and counting in the same language.

Initially, you may be asked to pay a premium for a business that is closely held, especially if it represents the life's work of the founder-owner. His attachment to his company may cause him to overestimate its value. There is a virtue if the ownership passes undiluted along to you: you will have full control to execute your business plan, and that might be a plus with your lenders.

Ultimately, however, you should expect to pay less in an insider buyout that you would on the open market for a comparable deal.

"Valuation is an art, not a science, but there are disciplines to follow," according to Irving L. Blackman, a Chicago attorney and CPA. [3]

Evaluating Businesses

To evaluate a business at the time of the owner's death, the IRS utilizes an eight-point checklist of factors including book value, earnings, past stock sales, and the general state of the economy. Major valuation firms require their appraisers to complete a checklist of 50 to 100 factors.

The larger the buyout proposed, the more likely headquarters is to bring in a third-party appraisal firm to perform a professional evaluation. Where two firms are involved, it is not unusual for their estimates to vary by 30 percent or more.

"The IRS itself emphasizes that the eight factors...do not have equal weight, and that valuation is a matter of judgment and common sense." Blackman said.

Some appraisers estimate a firm's value by taking an inventory of all the assets and then adding them up to find a replacement value.

Another way to estimate the value is to find the fair market value. Some appraisers do this by carefully evaluating in today's marketplace the whole list of tangible and intangible assets and then adding them up. Others ascertain market value by going out in the open market to seek offers for the firm as a package or to look for examples of comparable sales.

In a seller's market, the owners might optimistically set a price on their firm based on a combination of earnings, net tangible assets, and goodwill.

In an asset buyout, corporate financial officers may insist the value be based on book value.

Another, more likely way to evaluate a company in these times of leveraged buyouts is to figure how much in financing expenses the company can bear out of its cash flow. This assumes a reasonable rate of return and is undoubtedly a safer approach for the buyer than working from net worth or earnings figures.

You may have to spend a lot of time during the negotiations

listening to presentations by headquarters officials on why the price should be much higher than you are willing to pay. Listen patiently before you steer the conversation back to reality.

The reality of an insider buyout is that a realistic price is what the insider can afford to pay, not what an ideal prospect might pay if money and time were of no consequence.

Playing with the Price

Buyers beware. The sellers of small businesses often have "unrealistic expectations of what a buyer is willing to do," according to New York lawyer Stephen Rusmisel. [4]

And you are not in a position to be running around looking for some other business to buy.

Shareholders beware. The price of corporate spinoffs is usually low because often there is no competition in buying these small subsidiaries.

And headquarters is usually not in a mood to shop your division around.

But this much can be said for sure about the price scales in recent insider buyouts: all parties have had a good idea what they were doing and there has been next to no publicity about lingering price disputes.

In some insider buyouts the price on the deal almost seems to be a secondary issue.

In the Key Technology buyout from Applied Magnetics, Tom Madsen said negotiations lasted only "a couple of weeks on a verbal basis until we got down to the final strokes of what we might accept. Then a formal offer was made.

"The fact that we all knew one another from working with each other previously avoided the situation where someone went in and tried to [hoodwink] their way through.

"Applied Magnetics had a desire to sell the company, too, so we didn't have to debate that."

Madsen said the talks with Applied Magnetics went "reasonably well" in contrast to "some of these situations with ill feelings."

In our Garden Way Publishing buyout, I considered the meeting in Saratoga the most important moment of my life. This was going to be a dinner meeting with the entire executive committee, and I couldn't comfortably bring Don along, so I felt at a strategic disadvantage, if only in terms of numbers. Nervous as hell, I sat there drinking straight tonic water.

Finally, we talked about some substantive issues, including inventory and receivables valuations, properties that were included or excluded, key staff people that would be involved. We kicked around a couple of sticking points until everyone felt comfortable. Up to that point, we had been talking with headquarters for six weeks about an asset purchase. We thought all we needed to do was to define the value of the assets, to find a method of valuation that everyone agreed upon.

But a real surprise occurred when they came in with an asking price nearly 90 percent higher than what we intended to offer.

Their figure included full valuation on some mistakes we could not afford to pay for ourselves. One example was swollen inventories that would need to be heavily discounted to sell.

We had to say, "If that's it, we're out." The fact that we had not yet secured financing became an advantage to us at this point. Not that they felt sorry for us, but this was a reality they had to consider if they wanted to close the deal.

They said there might be a way for them to settle for less or maybe a way they could help finance the deal. "Come back with something that you can do," they suggested.

I went to my room for a couple of hours and prepared a logical, fair letter of response to their asking price. Then I called Don for his specific suggestions.

I met again with headquarters officials at 11 P.M. They chewed on our offer overnight. We met at 6:30 for breakfast and they said, "O.K. Let's do it."

After breakfast, we listed all our points of agreement and then called in a typist to prepare the letter of intent which we all signed.

Their original price had been close to book value and was a fair evaluation. If we had been instructed to take six months and sell the division on the open market, we probably could have gotten their price. On the other hand, in making the sales effort, the corporation could have spent or lost the difference and come out with some nasty, long-term wounds.

When all the evidence is in, the experts would probably agree that the fairest evaluation of an insider buyout is the price the parties agree to with their handshake.

Setting the Terms

It's an old custom in negotiations that the seller sets the price and the buyer sets the terms.

Although an insider buyout is another old custom (albeit with a new name), both buyers and sellers are likely to have a lot to say about both price and terms. In fact, an insider buyout may provide a situation for a complete role reversal, such as our Garden Way Publishing example.

Your terms will largely depend on the price and the way you structure your deal, but you need to be prepared for significant proposed changes during the final negotiations.

Some of these proposed changes may seem innocent but could threaten the very health of your future buyout. Last-minute changes may surface because they are obscure, which means they have been poorly researched. They could be a sign someone has had a change of heart.

It is easy for a crowd in negotiations, especially if groups of outside attorneys and accountants are involved, to lose sight of the overall mission of the talks and become bogged down in a morass of details about the terms.

Your main job as promoter of the deal is to continue to stage-manage the talks. Do not let your role as problem-solver become overshadowed by bit players. Do not let the buyout finale be too long delayed by changing the terms in the script.

Victor Kiam of Remington says the most important of the terms in a leveraged buyout transaction is "Time. Time to pay off the debt.

"The worst thing to happen to you is to have a gun at your head that you have to make a payback when you're not ready to do it.

"Once the sellers have sold the company, if they take back paper, all they are interested in is getting their loans repaid. If you fall behind, you are in a very difficult negotiating position. The lender can say, 'I'm sorry, I'm going to call my loan now and you sell your company to somebody else and give me the money.' You can lose everything.

"Maybe you have the cash. But if you take the cash out of the company, you can't do the things you wanted to do for the company.

"It's really key to finance yourself properly in your negotiations with the seller," Kiam said. "Try to stretch out your principal payments as long as possible so that you have the flexibility to operate."

Dick Hug, who bought Environmental Elements in July, 1983, said, "I was in a unique position. I was purchasing the company and still responsible for running the company for Koppers.

"The way our transaction was formulated in the letter of intent was that the closing operating statement and balance sheet would revert to November 1, 1982 [when his intentions to buy were confirmed].

"This sounds good on the surface. But the problem was I was still inhibited during negotiations from making changes, people changes that I wanted to make.

"We had a couple of sticky points during the final negotiations that took several sessions," Hug said. "Assumption of liability, pending lawsuits on workmen's compensation, some with merit, some without, things like that. We were trying to negotiate a split liability between us and Koppers, and because the extent of the liabilities was not known, obviously Koppers was not very amenable."

If the deal had fallen through, Hug's attorneys were worried they could be held responsible for the personnel changes.

"So in many respects, I did get a good start, but in many other respects, I was restrained until the final paper was signed," Hug said.

Negotiating Strategy

Eventually there comes a point when you stop being the trusted old division manager and become the corporation's sparring partner, or worse.

This will probably be after you have delivered your letter of intent and completed your preliminary buyout agreement with headquarters.

Things Change

This is when the exhilaration stage of the buyout ends. At this point you will be turned over to a transition or divestiture team of your peers for negotiations about specifics in the deal. This is the beginning of a war of nerves, a tough, exhausting, and frequently nasty period which may last from one to six months.

Your credibility begins to slip as you seem to be taking new positions on old assets and liabilities.

You are burdened with a mixed identity. You've been the one supposedly planning, organizing, directing, communicating, supporting, and analyzing for the company. Now it appears that you have been doing it instead on your own behalf.

You realize if the talks are not successful, you're out.

Your associates might look at you and wonder — or perhaps ask you directly — "If you're saying this equipment is worthless, why didn't you say this a few months ago?" If you think there's so much you can do to make the division better, how come you haven't done it before?"

In our buyout of Garden Way Publishing, we were all cooperatively, even happily, involved with the firm's top officers in thinking up creative ways to make our deal work. At this level we were treated as part of the solution.

Then we moved on to review details with finance, tax accounting, and warehousing, and suddenly we became part of the problem.

During this difficult period, some of the top officers became inaccessible. In one case, when we finally were "slid in" to a busy schedule, the meeting was limited to five minutes when we needed an hour.

However, the magic of an insider buyout is that it solves problems for both parties in a friendly, win-win way. That's your best position during negotiations and one that will be weakened if you focus on subsidiary factors.

"In a successful negotiation everybody wins," according to Gerard I. Nierenberg. "The objective should be to achieve agreement, not total victory. Both parties must feel that they have gained something." [5]

Points to Remember

Keep the negotiations fair, friendly, and non-confrontational. Be reasonable despite their responses. *Listen* to your counterparts.

Negotiate on the merits of the deal that will work to the best advantage of both sides. An insider buyout will only happen if both perceive they are coming out ahead.

Don't negotiate from too rigid a position.

Try to close the deal early.

We asked several persons to cite the most important thing to them in buyout negotiations.

"Hang tough for the key issues," said Vaughan Beals of Harley-Davidson. "Don't take the easy, expeditious way out."

Hanging tough, that's what Jerry Gura of Cherry Webb & Touraine was doing that Sunday evening after the Penn Square Bank went belly-up and his 50 percent partner called with a lending offer from an oil company which would have made him a 66 percent partner and reduced Gura to a 33 percent stake. Gura rejected the attempt to seize control of the deal and hung up.

Doug Baker, the Vermont innkeeper, said the most important thing in negotiations was, "One word, patience."

Patience is an unnerving sign of strength. Patience can serve to wear down and divide the other side and make an early resolution more important than the adoption of certain values or terms. It also provides time to probe and educate.

"You're in negotiations not only to win your own point but to come to some type of resolution to the situation, and usually there is a middle ground where you meet, and you have to learn to accept that middle ground," Baker said.

"You learn that in negotiations you always ask for more than what you really want...so that when you get to where you want to be, if the other side will give in a little, you'll actually come out a winner.

"A lot of people don't know that art — asking for more than you want — simply because most people are basically honest. They go into negotiations from a position they will have to give up. You can well afford to give up what you never expected to win," Baker said.

To complement and bolster your overall friendly, win-win negotiating strategy, you and your counselors must agree on the specific tactics you will use during the talks.

Our suggestions include the old favorites: Respond to their concerns. Meet their needs. Lead to their strengths. Invent options. Build trust. Act, don't react.

What these negotiating tips add up to is a process of getting all the facts and concerns out on the table where they can be discussed.

Additionally: keep your emotions and your ego in your briefcase. This is no time for loose cannons on the deck.

Also: be your own casting director. You're the reigning expert on the business on the table. Tell them how you are going to solve their problems.

Most important: use the ABC negotiating and sales technique: that's Always Be Closing.

If the negotiations take some surprising turns in an attempt, you suspect, to intimidate or pressure your side, don't reveal your anger or impatience. Remain true to your image of yourself as manager of sales, deals, and buyouts.

When the going gets tough, change the pace. Let your counselor take over and play tough for your side.

Regularly, during insider negotiations, you need to steer the conversation back to square one.

You might say, "Let's remember why we're sitting here — to solve these problems. It's true we seem far apart on this issue, who's going to pay for this. Let's go back to the fact that the corporation wants this to happen. Let's invent a solution to this problem.

"If you win this minor point, you might be threatening the very life of the new entity which would cause a public-relations problem and end the flow of cash back to the corporation."

If You Reach an Impasse

Be prepared for unexpected changes in the price or terms of the deal that could lead to a deadlock in your negotiations.

A deadlock can result when one side attempts to raise or lower the stakes. Or it can result from new information or perceptions that appear to change the balance.

Perceptions aside, deadlocks are real and can be costly in time and money.

One thing's for sure: it takes two sides to make a deadlock.

For the most part deadlocks will be the result of legitimate business issues. But insider buyouts are frequently fertile ground for deadlocks caused by emotional, petty, and not so petty personal and personality problems.

You should also watch for deadlocks that are imposed as a negotiating tactic to confuse you and wear down your patience.

The attorneys retained by headquarters may not have as benign a view of an insider buyout and insider friendships as the people you have been working with for years.

Don't Be Intimidated

Do not be intimidated by the threat of a collapse in the talks at this point. Approach deadlocks with patience by continuing to talk about solutions to the genuine problems of headquarters.

Be calm and confident, not cocky or combative. Try to appear relaxed. Study everybody's body language. Maintain friendly eye contact with those who have authority to close the deal. Break the ice: tell a family joke or arrange for your attorney to tease you about something trivial.

Ask Questions

Ask questions about the issue that has caused the deadlock. Listen carefully to the answers.

Don't focus on their statements of position. Probe to discover the reasoning behind their positions.

In your previous relationships with your superiors, your questions were answered directly with facts and recommendations. During negotiations, do not expect the same directness and quality of response now that you are almost an outsider.

Both sides can play this game. In an insider buyout deadlock, you are not obliged to bare your soul or provide a prompt reply as in an employer-employee relationship. Respectfully change the subject. Answer only a part of the question. Answer a different question. Ask for the question to be reworded or rephrase it to suit yourself. Or excuse yourself while you make an important telephone call back to the office.

Don't Get Cute

However, don't get too cute in an insider buyout. Continue to sell the strong points of your deal as if you were negotiating with a lender. Make your pitch to the sellers and steadfastly refrain from jousting and becoming competitive with their attorneys. The sellers are the only ones who have the authority to close the deal. This is not the time to become impatient or indignant.

Patiently try to discover the real reason for the deadlock by narrowing your focus. Is this an unexpected logjam or a planned stall imposed as a tactic to intimidate you and weaken your position? Offer to take the time to research and redefine the issues. Sometimes the threat of another delay is just the ticket for dissolving a deadlock.

Leave all the doors open. Don't burn any bridges. Find a way around the deadlock that will satisfy both sides.

You Can Yield

Be prepared to yield to reason and principle if the deadlock is warranted. But avoid being pressured into adding any sweeteners to the deal unless there is a quid pro quo.

Remain firm in the face of unwarranted pressure.

And never stray very far from your basic reasons for suggesting an insider buyout. Recall the original sentiments expressed by both parties.

Remind them that the goal of the talks is agreement in solving a mutual problem, not victory for one side or the other.

The stickiest, trickiest negotiations in our Garden Way Publishing buyout came just before the closing when headquarters announced its insistence that accounts receivable be included in the deal, a move that increased the price of the deal by over 250 percent.

Originally headquarters had wanted to collect these accounts, which was fine with us. Later, they realized this could be a mistake. In the crazy book publishing business, trade retailers are allowed to return unsold books for credit. What appears to a publisher as a receivable account may turn out to be old inventory and a cash liability. Headquarters had become concerned that without a publishing division, the company would have no way to process a stream of unsold books flowing back from retailers. The proportion of returned books to books sold may range from 10 to 30 percent.

The last-minute change in our deal meant enduring some negotiating over the value of the outstanding accounts, especially since we started talking with a 30 percent difference in the valuation of these accounts.

Our buying the accounts receivable meant we could open the mail on Day One and find checks enclosed. But the proportion also meant we were scurrying for additional last-minute financing and beginning our new business by focusing on past mistakes — ours and everyone else's — while we tried to collect old accounts.

The banker relationship was absolutely critical at this point. By now we had lined up financing, but it didn't include the receivables. We walked our banker-partner through the restructured deal, and after ten minutes, he said, "If the rest of the deal makes sense, this part makes real good sense." Knowing when to leave, we left.

Relationships Change

The relationship with Koppers didn't begin to get touchy until April, Dick Hug said of his July, 1983 buyout of Environmental Elements from Koppers.

"Until then, our relationship was good. But when we got down to the nitty-gritty negotiations, obviously I wanted to get as good a deal as I could, and they in turn...got a little bit testy. I began to wonder whether this thing was going to work. Then, on the other side of the fence, there was a lot of wondering on the part of Koppers people whether they ought to sell this business."

It was at this point that a memo that Hug had written came back to haunt him during the final negotiations:

"Several months before this began [in September 1982], I had written a five- or six-page memorandum to the president and chairman of the company telling them why they should not sell the Environmental business — for all the reasons that I bought the Environmental business. The future was there. The position we had in the marketplace. Our technology.

"I gave them facts, figures, forecasts, and performances. I think the longer this thing played out, the longer they had to think about it. They began to wonder if this was the right decision.

"If we had not completed our deal in July [1983] as we did, it may never have closed."

Closing the Deal

Remember, closing the deal is in effect closing the sale. This is no time to relax and give up your responsibility as sales manager for the deal. This is the time for you to move into your new role as the president, chief public spokesman, and sales manager for your new company.

Meanwhile your attorney will be responsible for preparing all the necessary acquisition agreements and documents.

However, in your haste to get on with running your new company, be sensitive to your attorney's concerns about tying up all loose ends of the deal. Hold the handshakes and champagne until your attorney signals he is satisfied all the specifics have been met.

The final day of negotiations in Dick Hug's buyout of Environmental Elements from Koppers began in the attorneys' offices at 10 A.M. and continued until the final papers were signed at 6:30 A.M. the following morning. "It was all day and all night."

However long the negotiations take, two weeks or two years, it's as Dick Snyder said: "My position was, I had to get the keys."

No Losers

Then, when all is said, signed, and transferred, congratulate the sellers. Make them believe they won. Because if you and your counselors did it right, there will be no losers among the parties in an insider buyout.

"We learned something," Jerry Gura said. "They are not all barracudas out there. When you're really giving it your all, when you've maintained your integrity with people, the people you do business with are very supportive. They are not out to rape you. There's always an exception — and we had a couple. But generally they lined up behind you and they cheered for you. It was terrific."

In our case, the closing was an anticlimax. The homework had been done thoroughly on both sides. Two checks were drawn. I signed five papers and went home and kissed my wife.

Chapter VIII References:

[1] "Corporate Divestiture: The Seller's Viewpoint," by Leslie M. Frecon, manager of acquisitions, General Mills, Inc., *The Journal of Buyouts and Acquisitions,* August 1983.

[2] "They Called in the Texans, Risked Every Cent, Then Won," Emilia Askari, *Miami Herald,* November 28, 1983.

[3] "What's Your Business Worth?" by Irving Blackman, SBA photocopy from *Inc.).*

[4] *The Wall Street Journal,* August 20, 1984.

[5] Gerard I. Nierenberg, *The Art of Negotiating,* Hawthorne Books, Inc., 1968.

Chapter IX

Financing the Buyout

Gather together ten individuals who would like to try insider buyouts. Ask them to rank, in order of difficulty, the problems they'll face. Chances are that eight or more of them will put financing at the top of the lists.

Ask ten people who have successfully negotiated insider buyouts to do the same thing, and chances are that eight or more will rank finances way down the lists.

The conclusion you should draw from this: if your deal is a sound one, the money is out there waiting for you.

A further conclusion: financial backing may be available from a source you might not consider — your parent company.

Raising money to finance our insider buyout at Garden Way Publishing required hard work and careful planning, but at no time was it seen as an insurmountable difficulty. Is this true of most insider buyouts or were we just plain lucky?

We asked a few others involved in buyouts. Here are a few of the replies:

Victor Kiam, Remington Products: "A lot of managers don't think they can do it, but there is a lot of money around."

Tom Begel, Pullman Transportation Co.: "The financing is the easiest part. There is an amazing amount of money available.... There are people we talk to in New York who continually say there is more money chasing deals than there are deals chasing money. This has been true for the past year or two and I think it will continue to be true.

"What everybody is looking for is the right manager in the right company. Once you've got that combination, money is the least of their concerns."

To be successful in raising the funds, you must be able to convince those with money that you understand the business — the product, the manufacturing process, the market, the finances that make it all happen.

Be complete when describing your needs for funds. Lenders will understand that you need money both to acquire the business and to have working capital. Your request for funds should include both needs. A request for acquisition funds alone may indicate to lenders that you don't fully appreciate the finances of the business you're moving into.

Again, we received backing from others on this approach.

Lou Auletta, Bauer/Electro: "Make sure you have enough money in your financing package going forward to establish a decent line of credit both to grow with and to take care of the unforeseen situations."

Vaughan L. Beals, Harley-Davidson Motor Co.: "Make sure [your financing package] covers worst-case [conditions] — and that should be worse than you can conceive."

And, finally, as you address this question of raising money, the presentation you make to prospective lenders can make or break you, no matter how good your deal may be. A slipshod presentation will convince lenders that your presentation reflects your attitude toward the business. You can't put too much time and effort into this crucial step in the execution of the insider buyout.

Writing Your Business Plan

Bankers will expect you to present them a business plan before you even discuss a loan with them. This plan, you must remember, will serve several functions:

1. It will tell lenders whether you have the talent and understanding of the business required to make it a success. If the plan is good, it will guarantee you an audience with the lenders.

2. It will outline in detail your financial needs.

3. And often the most important, it will define for you what this business is that you plan to create. By putting it all down on paper, you will clarify this for yourself and perhaps even discover — before the lenders do — weak points in your planning.

In Chapter V, you'll remember, we discussed how your division's management plans evolved into your insider buyout plan, a transition plan you used to describe your buyout proposal to headquarters.

Your insider buyout plan now evolves into a broader and more detailed plan—your business plan—which you will use to describe your business to outsiders.

Drafting this latest plan will force you to review your specific objectives and articulate your assumptions. It is all part of a continuing process of self-education and sharing.

You need to redocument and repackage your knowledge of the business for the growing number of people with whom you will be establishing business relationships. Your "new" suppliers will want to see this.

Your business plan should include all relevant information presented in an informative, promotional, and easy-to-follow style and format.

"Mine came out to be about 150 pages including complete pro formas," said Dick Snyder of Snyder General Corp. "It talked about the competitive marketplace, the economic environment, state of the art products, where the company stands."

The Right Timing

When you prepare your polished business plan depends upon when you need to secure your financing commitments. Your timing needs to be carefully considered. Prepare your business plan too soon and it will appear stale and dated. Prepare it too late and you may miss your buyout deadline.

In our case, we signed the letter of intention with Garden Way,

Inc. on May 3, 1983, and I delivered a 100-page prospectus and business plan to five bankers on May 13. I'm sure I worked 300 hours in those ten days.

Snyder says, "You need to have first-class presentation for the financial community. You've got to put together a strong business plan that looks professional and is professional."

This does not mean your business plan needs to be processed by a professional business plan writer. But it absolutely requires the heart, soul, and imprint of a professional business manager.

Get Reviews

Buyout managers should write their own business plans, but invite all counselors, advisors, and consultants to review and critique the plan for omissions, confusions, and redundancies. Get it drafted and on the table so you can sit with your counselors, rip it to shreds, and then knit it back together in an improved fashion.

Clearly, a personal computer and word processor keep this from becoming an unmanageable process. In our case, we found an erroneous assumption that changed every financial sheet in the plan. We found this on the date we were scheduled to give the plan to the bankers, but we met our deadline.

After yourself, the most important target audience for your business plan is your lenders. Bankers use business plans to measure how well prospective borrowers know their businesses. It's a way to evaluate management, products, markets, and cash flow. It's like a written exam.

Bankers wonder about prospective borrowers: will they have enough capital, labor, and marketing tools? Have they anticipated the problems of ownership? Will they be able to teach me anything? The business plan should answer these questions.

Most buyout managers agree business plans should be delivered only to a few selected lending institutions in care of a friend or a friend-of-a-friend after an introductory call.

"You wouldn't believe the shoddy business plans we get in here," said Stanley M. Pechman, president of a White Plains, New York, small-business investment company, "Frankly, most of them go right in the wastebasket." [1]

"Ninety-nine out of 100 business plans that are received by venture capitalists are never funded....only about 10 percent of those plans make it past first reading, and only 10 percent of those are ever funded," according to Sabin Russell of *Venture* magazine. [2]

Russell continued, "Venture capitalists are not impressed with computer-generated scenarios in business plans."

Balanced Pro Formas

To preserve credibility, the pro formas should be neither optimistic nor conservative, according to Ernst & Whinney consultants. "The plan should present a most-likely scenario that has a 60 percent chance of success, with optimistic and pessimistic scenarios that have 20 percent chances of occurring." [3]

Some bankers measure it by its weight.

Russell said lenders told him a business plan "that is no more than one-quarter to one-half inch thick, loosely bound in a clear plastic cover, will do nicely."

'Crisp' Is Target

Write your business plan "clearly and concisely," Russell said. "The word venture capitalists most love to describe a good business plan is 'crisp'."

But however thick or thin you write your business plan, prepare a fresh, individually typed copy with custom-prepared pages for each prospective lender to suit his particular orientation.

Russell J. Warren of the Ernst & Whinney accounting and business consulting firm said: "The importance of the business plan as a source of useful information cannot be overemphasized....

"It becomes both the key marketing document for obtaining financing and a road map for running the business afterwards....

"Like a job-seeker's resume, a business plan's purpose in life is to secure an interview for its writer."

As with resumes, there is no standard, universally accepted format for your business plan.

Write, rewrite, organize, and reorganize your plan for readability, easy comprehension, and sales appeal.

Prepare your plan to be convincing, not conforming.

Writing Your Business Plan

Here is a comprehensive list of subjects to consider including in your business plan. Begin by collecting notes and reports in a ring-binder. Don't use two pages where one will do. Rewrite your summaries and column headings to suit your audience. Continue to collate and condense until the cream rises to the surface. [4]

1. Cover page. Name, address, and telephone numbers of the business to be financed and the buyer submitting the proposal.

2. Table of Contents.

3. Introduction. A management overview. A one- or two-page summary of the proposal including mission, goals, and markets of the business. Economic impact upon the region. Outline of financing plans for the buyout and the business. Highlights of management's strengths, philosophy, and commitment. Why business is for sale and why management wants to buy it.

4. Management Resources. Brief resumes of the experience and skills of the manager-buyer(s). Compensation before and after the buyout. Equity commitments. Summary of plans for reorganization and management development. Professional services and counselors. Management references.

5. Business Descriptions. Locations. Products and services. Market niche and distribution. Skills and labor. Raw materials and suppliers. Key operating policies. Operating environment (geographic, government, labor, cultural, political). Available and emerging technology. Detailed history.

6. Market Analyses. Customer base and details of potential. Major competitors and market share. Major threats and opportunities. Feasibility studies, existing or planned. Industry history and five-year outlook.

7. Strategic Plans. Philosophy, plans, and goals for financing, sales and marketing, production, research, new product development, capital spending, and organizational development.

8. Buyout Timetables. Schedules for securing financing, transferring ownership, start-up or transfer times, fiscal year, significant annual operating events, and rationale for timing. Pay particular attention to this. Our eventual banker was most impressed with the calendar we assembled and held us to it. Several times he commented, "You haven't missed a date yet." This is important to any lender.

9. Buyout Finance Plan. Estimated value of the business. Schedule of assets including current appraisals of fixed assets, collateral, owner equity, other equity. Debt financing needed. Capital and debt service requirements and plans. Credit history and references.

10. Financial Statements. Three to five years of income statements, balance sheets, and critical ratios.

11. Pro Forma Financials. Projected operating statements, balance sheets, earnings, cash flows, sales and shipments, and other performance reports for the period covering the longest debt.

12. For More Information. One page with names and addresses of the seller, other principals participating in the buyout, and professional firms associated with both parties. References (which should be checked). Find out, afterwards, which ones were checked and thank them for their help.

13. Index. One page with up to fifty key subjects and financial totals listed by page or cross-referenced to sections as listed in the Table of Contents.

Controlling Your Financing

One of the promises of an insider buyout is the chance to seize control of your life.

The easiest way to keep control is to limit the number of people who have equity in your deal. Cut the deal down to a size you can finance alone or with a small group.

"We wanted to keep control over the operations of the company ourselves," said Tom Madsen of Key Technology.

"The four of us in the management group had talked to some venture capital people. But one of our partners had been involved in a small deal down in southern California and he was somewhat soured on getting that type of company involved.

"We were concerned that if we were to bring in venture capitalists, with our not having a lot of equity to put up ourselves, we might get too much involvement from outsiders in the operations of the company," Madsen said.

Leverage is an alternative to equity.

Leverage means debt financing as opposed to equity financing.

Debt financing is asset-based, collateralized financing.

More borrowing and more leverage usually means less dilution of control for the buyers. Leverage helps a buyer stretch the power of personal financial and management resources to the fullest. Managers with limited personal resources who want to keep control of their insider buyout will want to consider a highly leveraged purchase.

A leveraged buyout is a way to leverage managerial skills and experience instead of sitting back and allowing outside equity players to come in and dominate the deal.

Less Cash Needed

A little capital goes a long way in a leveraged buyout, especially in an insider buyout.

Many LBOs are written for five years with quarterly interest and principal payments. Some call for only interest payments in the early years with one principal payment at the end of the term.

Less leverage means the buyers need proportionately more equity. This could lead to dilution of control if the buyers' resources are limited. The more money taken in from outside investors, the less the control of the insiders.

Deals based on cash flow may need to rely upon shorter-term, secondary lenders or equity players who may want out in five or so years.

In many larger firms, where the goal is wealth, not personal control, a merger or a public offering may lie at the end of the term as a way to pay the backers and any lenders.

"The major objective of many entrepreneurs (so stated in many business plans) is to go public." This from Arthur Lipper III, chairman of *Venture* magazine. [5]

Not Our Aim

By contrast, our definition of an entrepreneur is not someone who aspires to sell out and work for a public firm. My intention from the beginning was to maintain as much equity as possible in my new corporation, reserving stock for key managers. Two years into the venture I still have 100 percent.

We mention the public-offering and merger options in which personal wealth is a goal, not by way of recommendation, but by way of contrast to an insider buyout where the satisfaction of gaining and retaining control of your personal and business life is a thrill and a goal.

Meanwhile, your insider buyout is likely to be a package of interdependent debt and equity commitments from three or more of the major sources of buyout financing explained below. These financing sources are listed in order of diminishing control for the buyer.

Manager's Equity

Manager's equity is your personal savings and assets which are used as security for loan guarantees. Such assets might include your home, certificates of deposit, securities, and personal notes from relatives, friends, or the seller.

This is scary, but don't become petrified with fear. You'll almost certainly be asked for a personal guarantee, which will include your house and such emotionally charged items such as your wife's rings, but the bankers really don't want to march up your driveway — at least ours didn't.

Also, you may own stock in the company and have earned vested pension credits. You are most likely entitled to severance pay, bonuses, and other cash items. All of these are a part of your assets.

"IPOs [initial public stock offerings] and venture capital represent the most conspicuous — but not the most significant — sources of funds for entrepreneurs," according to *Venture* magazine's Kevin Farrell. "Far more businesses are brought to life with personal savings." [6]

Since 1980, the amount of personal savings used to fund business start-ups and buyouts has grown nearly 55 percent. In 1984, this totaled $775 billion.

In the buyout by four managers of Key Technology from Applied Magnetics, President Tom Madsen said, "Basically we just funded it out of our own savings....We knew that Harold Frank [Applied Magnetic's chairman] might play the role of venture capitalist. Applied Magnetics also carried a note.

"We were also able to arrange long-term financing with a bank in Los Angeles, First Interstate, which Harold and [a sixth partner], Ed Shannon, arranged. If it had not been for them, we could not have guaranteed that note based on the net worth of the four principals here."

Commercial Lenders

These are fixed-rate, long-term, asset-based lenders such as banks, insurance companies, and pension funds.

In a large leveraged deal, these major lenders are likely to require you to secure debt or equity commitments from one or more of the other sources listed below by way of spreading the risk and adding to the overall scrutiny of the deal. It becomes a matter of how much control you have to give up to satisfy your banker or partner.

Some major commercial lenders are directly affiliated with venture capital firms which they will want as equity players.

Making the rounds of the banks is like a trip to never-never land. You lay your business plan on someone's desk, and he doesn't know what you're talking about. He's never heard of your top products.

He's looking at you. You're looking at him. And you're not talking the same language. It's eerie.

Large banks can be impressive, but the fit may not be exactly right. The Bank of New England in Boston knew a lot about publishing, marketing, and direct mail. Its officials liked our business plan but rejected our loan proposal because it was too modest. They invited us to come back "if you ever need some really big money."

The manager of the local bank we borrowed from, First Vermont in Bennington, Vermont, seemed to have the most local autonomy and the most on the ball. Others would call each week to apologize for delays in reviewing our proposals.

Almost instantaneously, during this difficult period, our banker, Knute Westerlund, became a close friend. It was almost a jovial, joyous relationship.

To find that kind of a banking friend, "you've got to knock on an awful lot of doors," Dick Snyder said of the commercial lenders.

For example, in 1983, Bob Phillips, Gary Edman, and Charles Stewart wanted to buy out the Chambers Belt Co. from The Victorio Co. in Phoenix.

"We really didn't know what we were going to do," Phillips told Bruce G. Posner of *Inc.* magazine. "We didn't know where to start, and we only had about two weeks to pull everything together." [7]

"We learned that there were a lot of sharks out there," Erdman said.

The trio received no encouragement from the Phoenix banks until they met Vice President John Hansgen, of the Thunderbird Bank. In a few minutes one evening, Hansgen suggested a plan for raising $4 million, including a $550,000 Small Business Administration loan collateralized by equipment and a $1.4 million Thunderbird loan against the value of inventory.

Hansgen also suggested a second bank loan on the accounts receivable worth $1.5 million and promised to find another bank to share the risk. He also helped plan for new mortgages on the trio's homes and within a couple of days had recruited four private investors with $600,000 who took 15 percent of the company. In three weeks the deal was signed and closed.

Economic Development Programs

Economic development programs are sponsored by various federal, state, or local government agencies and include loans, loan guarantees, tax benefits, employee training, and a great variety of other economic development provisions including:

1. Small Business Investment Companies (SBICs) and Minority Enterprise Small Business Investment Companies (MESBICs) — equity players who borrow from the Small Business Administration.

These are usually local or regional development corporations organized by business leaders and then licensed and regulated by the SBA as a source of long-term, subordinated, venture-capital equity financing for small businesses. They take up to a 49 percent equity position.

Because the SBIC - guaranteed financing is considered equity, it is especially useful in leveraging more debt financing.

The SBIC terms are generous with only interest payments scheduled during the early payback years and with lower interest and collateral requirements than conventional loans.

The development goals of the SBICs will vary from region to region, serving in some cases to bring in new industry and striving in other areas to save established employers.

The definition of a small business varies for each industry, but a small manufacturer according to SBIC guidelines is one with fewer than 1,500 employees.

2. The Small Business Administration, nicknamed "the business lender of last resort," guarantees loans for up to 90 percent in deals under $500,000. But watch out, the SBA packages are unusually credit restrictive for a growth company.

3. Other federal, state, and local government agencies.

State economic development agencies are usually the best source of information about available government programs which may range from federal job training to state aid for depressed areas to local tax stabilization.

Seller Financing

Seller financing uses the savings and personal assets of one or more individuals selling you their business. More often, it involves the varied assets and resources of a corporate seller, the very assets and resources you have spent years managing.

These resources may include cash, loan guarantees, securities, real estate, equipment, inventory, royalties, rights, and any number of other valuable considerations that might help float a business divestiture.

Seller financing is often readily available in an insider buyout. You are a known quantity. This is a friendly deal. The commitment by headquarters to the business may not be wholehearted, but it should be sufficient to extend you credit.

Banks love this show of faith in management.

"If you're going to do a buyout, find out how much paper you can get from the owner," said the Vermont innkeeper, State Senator Doug Baker.

"If there's an existing mortgage, try to assume the mortgage and then split the differences on the balance with the owner if possible, paying cash for half and possibly taking paper on the other half. It gives you a better ability to work for cash flow," Baker said.

In a buyout, the seller benefits from tax-code provisions allowing installment sales without immediate tax consequence. What's more, the seller is more likely to approve an installment sale with an inside manager than with an outside party.

The sellers are willing to lend on a guaranteed basis because they know the assets; you miss a payment and they can send someone over to run the shop and collect on the accounts receivable until they're paid off.

Norman Dion, chairman and founder of Dysan Corp., manufacturer of discs and other computer equipment, is a strong advocate of parent-company financing for employee buyouts and start-ups as means for:

1. Stopping pirating of key employees by competitors.

2. Preventing competition from employee start-ups.

3. Providing affiliated sources of outside research and development.

4. Preserving a small company atmosphere.

5. "Making a lot of rich friends." [8]

In this spirit, Control Data Corp. of Minneapolis has invested in more than seventy high-tech start-ups involving former employees. [9]

But for a record of cooperation between the parent company and an insider buyer, who can top the sale by IMS International Inc., the New York-based pharmaceutical research firm, of its American microcomputer sales and leasing division to its chief financial officer for $1, and a similar French operation to the French managers for one franc? [10]

Insider Financing

Insider financing refers to the use of the savings and personal assets of employees, directors, sub-contractors, and other close business associates who are not principals of the buyout group. This is not a start-up source of funds.

Such financing may be either equity or debt, that is, either investments in securities or cash for loans and notes.

"For many cash-poor start-ups, offering stock for services in lieu of hard currency...is often used to create a sound and relatively cheap insurance policy against the defection of top personnel," according to *Inc.* magazine. [11]

Another way to tap insider savings without necessarily sacrificing control is through variations on Employee Stock Option Plans (ESOPs).

ESOPs are ordinarily a way for workers to obtain shares in the company that employs them. The ESOP plans are similar to pension or profit-sharing programs in which firms may deduct contributions to them from taxable earnings. All employees in firms with ESOPs generally own shares according to seniority, but usually the employee holdings are not large enough to be a threat to management control of the firm.

Many of the ESOPs are managed by Kelso & Co., whose founder, Louis Kelso, invented and pioneered the technique thirty years ago.

Lately, existing ESOPs are being used increasingly by management groups as partial financing of their buyouts.

Dentsply International of York, Pennsylvania, a dental supplies firm, went private in 1982 with equity split between the Dentsply ESOP, 36 percent; management, 35 percent; Kelso & Co., 5 percent; and purchasers of subordinated debentures, 24 percent.

ESOPs got a big boost from 1984 tax changes effective in 1985. These require banks to pay taxes on only 50 percent of the interest income they receive on loans to ESOPs when the loans are used to buy stock from company owners. This translates into lower borrowing costs for employee groups doing a company buyout. [12]

Partners' Equity

Partners' equity is the savings and personal assets of your friends and business associates, including other members of your insider management buyout team, members of your new board of directors, and passive or silent partners such as friends, relatives, or advisors.

Be careful here. You can lose control of your deal and your business just as quickly with friends and other insiders as you can with outsiders and venture capitalists.

Victor Kiam of Remington gives this example of how a manager may begin to lose control of the business with partners:

"Let's say you're the president of XY Division of the Mammoth Corporation. Your marketing guy starts to slow up and you decide you want to make a change. You either make the change unilaterally or you go to the corporation and they make the change. Either way, the guy is gone.

"Now [after an insider buyout], you find out he's one of your stockholders.

"You've got to make sure that those people who are getting a piece of the action are the people you want with the company for ten years.

"On the other side of the coin, giving them a piece of the action, if they are good...there's less likelihood of them leaving.

"One of the key elements is rapport — whether the money is available or not. If you don't have rapport with the chap that you're dealing with...don't get involved," Kiam said.

"You need a basic solid relationship because you are going to be married for five or ten years....But you need to have the same mutual goals and mutual respect.

"If [the business after the buyout] is a failure, everybody's in the same boat and you try to come out as best you can. But if it does well, there will be divergent opinions about what to do next....You will have about nineteen thousand different ideas about what to do. You've got to be sure you have somebody who is in complete sympathy with you," Kiam said.

Venture Capital

Venture capital is the personal or corporate resources of outside investors who are willing to accept risk for a high return.

The investors may be passive or they may be active, eager to become involved in management to meet their goals.

The variety of public and private corporations that engage in providing equity capital is limitless, but the list includes conglomerates, insurance companies, foreign corporations, and, most notably, investment banks and venture capitalists.

Venture capitalists and other outside investors purchase their equity in the form of common stock, preferred stock, convertible stock, or stock with stock warrants.

The relationship between the outside investors and the management-buyers may range from a close partnership to a passive funding role, or from a majority of seats on the board of directors to a teaching role.

Some feel that the first step in doing a buyout is to find a good investment banker, someone who has no existing ties to the corporation and who has been recommended by a friend, or a friend of a friend.

Venture capitalists are looking for capital gains. They want to turn over their portfolios at about five-year intervals and look for a gain of seven to ten times their original investment.

They have a tendency to want to go public or sell the business to a larger firm. Management risks losing control of the business with heavy venture capital participation.

There are now nearly 700 venture capital funds seeking long-term growth-oriented investors. The funds may be legally organized as a business development corporation (BDC), a small-business investment company (SBIC), or a public venture capital partnership. [13]

Vermont and Massachusetts, where we chose to work and operate, have a large number of state and local development corporations which looked quite attractive to us at the onset, but which were, in the end, not required to make the financing work.

Industry observers predict the venture capital boom, which began in 1978 with reduced taxes on capital gains taxes, will not last, especially if taxes are raised again to help fund the federal budget deficits.

Going Public

Going public is raising capital by selling shares of the business to investors in the stock markets.

Although most division buyouts are staged by managers eager to become independent entrepreneurs, some are staged with the idea of selling all or most of the equity in a few years to another firm or to investors in the stock markets. The cash generated is used to expand, to strengthen the balance sheet by removing leveraged debt, and to pay off the managers-owners at a profit.

Preparing to go public is costly in time and fees, and it erodes many of the entrepreneurial incentives that created the business in the first place.

This is not the route we advocate for inside managers who want to retain maximum control of their buyouts. Don't exchange one boss for another.

In a typical small insider buyout of corporate assets in a mundane division, there will not be the growth rates that would suit an initial public stock offering. While this move is worth checking out and knowing about, it's unlikely to become attractive to stock purchasers until there is a steady stream of annual earnings for the new company.

Shopping for Lenders

The most important ingredient of your financing package is the money. First, find the money.

Less important are the terms. But arranging the terms will probably be the most difficult part of negotiating the funding for your deal. Nonetheless, postpone negotiating the terms until the money is secured.

Don't worry too much about the interest rates. The real costs of interest, after taxes, can range from zero to only 6 to 8 percent in the case of a profitable firm paying 12 to 16 percent.

Frequently, cash flow provided by restructured depreciation allowances after the sale is sufficient to cover the debt service of the buyout.

Whom should a manager thinking of a buyout see first about financing? We asked Victor Kiam of Remington Products this question.

"Go to your local bank first," Kiam said. "Seek out people in the community who are the leaders."

Most likely, it is these community leaders who are the founders and directors of your local small-business investment company (SBIC).

Lou Auletta said the financing of his buyout of Bauer/Electro was arranged through account executives with banks in the Hartford area.

"It took us a little bit of shopping around because we needed someone who has an appreciation of our business — the pitfalls and unique situations. We are a major capital-equipment manufacturer: you can look at the balance sheet one month and see a relatively good profit, and the next month, because the product did not go out the door, we could be showing a cash deficiency. Getting the bank or the lender to understand the value of the business is extremely important."

Looking for money to fund his computer-controlled Repair Management Systems Corp., Harold C. Ruff Jr. of Philadelphia struck out with the banks, the SBA, and venture capitalists before associating with a small business investment company.

Ruff said the "nightmare" taught him, "It isn't what you're doing, or what you're trying to sell, but who it is you've got telling your story for you. I got nothing until I hooked up with people who knew other people who had money." [13]

Guidelines for buyout dealmaking were developed by Bill Moore, president of the Houston-based Moorco International Inc., which he formed from six manufacturing businesses bought from Geosource, a subsidiary of Aetna Life & Casualty Co.

Moore's exciting story, along with two dozen others and articles by professional buyout experts and analysts, appears in the case history digest, *Structuring and Financing Management Buyouts,* one of a series by Buyout Publications of San Diego. [13]

Moore and other top managers realized their "lifetime goal of running their own shows" in a $140 million deal that was expected to gross $200 million in 1984. That's a very big deal from the perspective of this book.

Moore concluded his big buyout in Houston during June, 1984. From a look at a few of Moore's rules reprinted below, you would think we had been sharing our notes with him.

• Control the deal yourself. Do not allow key decisions to be made on your behalf by others.

• Undertake concurrent negotiations with multiple lenders and underwriters.

• Negotiate comprehensive engagement letters early and get them in writing.

• Do not give any organization an exclusive right to raise debt or equity.

• Restrict complete responsibility for all aspects of the deal to as few individuals as possible.

- Control the formation of and appointments to the board.
- Work with your advisors in selecting the equity investors.
- Retain the finest professional assistance available, regardless of the cost.

Had Commitments Early

In taking Unitog private in a management buyout, Bob Hagans and his venture capitalist, G. Kenneth Baum, received commitments from three banks before announcing their tender offer. Because of the necessity for speed and secrecy in buying out a public company, they restricted their financing search to "dictator banks — the one-man banks" that make loans on the approval of the chief executive officer without the time-consuming need to gain committee approval.

One of the banks, Hagans said, was a Kansas City bank that specialized in commercial and real-estate loans, but had never done an industrial deal. Hagans said the bank used their entrée into the world of corporate buyouts as a way to announce: "Hey guys, there's another bank in town."

"We had four banks," said Dick Snyder of Snyder General Corp. "The lead bank was Texas Mercantile Corporation. They did the documentation and had three participants. I had known Mercantile because it is a Dallas-based bank and they knew me fairly well. But they spent a lot of time reviewing and evaluating [our proposal]. Banks who do secured lending not only look at the collateral and the assets but also at the management of the company."

Also participating in the Snyder General financing were two small-business investment companies, one, the Mercantile and the other from an Oklahoma City bank.

"They were not essential in doing the deal. They were to a great extent cosmetic....The type of money they bring in is equity money," Snyder said. "Singer management was a little leery of doing it on 100 percent debt. So they wanted some comfort from some deep-pocket players."

And a Midwest banker who saw a bank buyout by his bank's board of directors collapse offers this word of caution about lenders, including your bank: "Double check the stability of your lender. Make sure he isn't a candidate for Chapter 11. Don't put your finances all in one basket as we did.

"We were the victims of bad timing...changes in the banking economy....The future of independent banks? That's a time that's past...."

One thing we learned was that first impressions of bankers can be very telling — and very accurate. What you see at the very outset is what you tend to get. And the first one back to you with more questions, and interest, may wind up being your long-term banker.

Living with Your Lenders

You're always working for someone, and in an insider buyout, if it's not your board of directors, it is likely to be your lenders.

Keep your bankers deeply involved in your business. Give them more data than they ask for.

And share your visions fully with more than one lender.

Lou Auletta of Bauer/Electro told how he stays in touch with his bankers: "They make periodic visits just out of interest, just to see what's happening. We provide them with monthly statements so that they have an idea what's happening."

Milton Deaner, the president of McLouth Steel Products, which he rescued from bankruptcy court in 1982, talked about the need to be honest with lenders:

"I came over here [to Detroit] totally unprepared. I am a technical person with no financial training whatsoever. But suddenly I have a bankrupt company doing $500 to $600 million a year in business....

"My job was to keep the interest of the secured lenders from liquidating, to demonstrate to them that we were not eroding their equity, that in the long term they would get more return by letting us stay in business.

"You've got to get along with your secured lenders....You have to be honest....You just have to make certain that you have credibility....Try to be honest regardless of the circumstances....If the news is bad, give it, don't try to hide it."

Chapter IX References:

[1] "The Trick To Selling A Small Deal," by Kevin Farrell, *Venture,* October 1984.

[2] "What Investors Hate Most About Business Plans," Sabin Russell, *Venture,* June 1984.

[3] "Business Packages: Their Preparation and Presentation," by Frank S. Novak and Kathy E. Ruekberg, Ernst & Whinney, Cleveland; in *The Journal of Buyouts & Acquisitions,* August-September 1984.

[4] Business plan contents suggested by Charles Abbott & Associates, Elmhurst, N.Y.

[5] "Chairman's Comments," by Arthur Lipper III, chairman, *Venture* magazine, April 1985.

[6] "There's No Stopping Now," by Kevin Farrell, *Venture,* February 1985.

[7] By Bruce G. Posner, *Inc.* magazine, September 1984.

[8] "Millionaire Maker," by Roger Neal, *Forbes,* September 12, 1983.

[9] "When a Former Employer Backs Your Startup," by Richard Barbieri, *Venture,* November 1983.

[10] "Prescription Counter: IMS, Researcher for Drug Houses, Sheds Money Losers," *Barron's,* October 29, 1984.

[11] "Putting Stock in Your Advisors," by Joseph P. Kahn, *Inc.* magazine, June 1984.

[12] "Kelsonomics in Theory and Practice," by Michael Hoyt, *Venture,* January 1985.

[13] *Structuring and Financing Management Buyouts,* L. Ryder Mason, Buyout Publications, 1984.

Chapter X

Managing on Your Own

You have closed your insider buyout and it's a success. Now it is day one of your reborn business with you as the new owner. You are up and running on your own.

Be prepared for changes. I drove up to my new Storey Communications worldwide headquarters on Day One, and started the day by driving squirrels out of our reception area.

But it's worth it. Your buyout will create some exciting changes in your life. The highs will be higher, and the lows will be lower. You will always remember the agony and the ecstasy of your first ninety days.

"I think everyone in the organization takes more pride," said Victor Kiam of his Remington Products buyout. "They are in a stand-alone outfit now. They are making their own way. They know they've got problems, but, by God, they're doing it on their own. They don't have big daddy down the street calling the shots.

"If more than one manager participates in this [buyout], there is a feeling of togetherness and ownership that extends downward into the organization.

"If the top five or six managers are participating, you've got a group pulling toward similar ends instead of hired hands without a stake.

"You'd be surprised how the hours worked per day go up when somebody has a piece of the action. They worked eight hours before, now [after the buyout] they work ten or twelve."

"I think it brought out the best in all of us," Vermont State

Senator Douglas J. Baker said of his family partnership buyout of the Sugarhouse Motor Inn & Restaurant.

"My own personal feelings about myself, my own self worth, went up five hundred percent," Baker said. "I found I had abilities I didn't even know existed."

Sleeps Better

"I tend to sleep a whole lot better. I'm running my own show and master of my own destiny," said Richard E. Hug of Environmental Elements. "I don't have to worry about going to this meeting and that meeting and reporting to somebody in Pittsburgh. I feel a hell of a lot better."

When John T. Mahoney finished signing and exchanging documents at the closing of his 1983 buyout of TransLogic Corp., attorneys cheered and champagne was opened in celebration. Mahoney sipped one glass — then rushed back to the factory.

"Suddenly it was our buildings, machinery, and payroll," Mahoney explained. [1]

Three Benefits

Jerry Gura, CWT Specialty Stores, put it this way:

"I have not really changed my intensive work routine, but I have enjoyed three great psychological benefits.

"The enjoyment of being an entrepreneur.

"A growth in personal net worth.

"And a measurable feeling of security."

Coping with Unexpected Hazards

There are going to be surprises. In our case, a ten-year paper supplier greeted our news of the exciting buyout by asking for $90,000 up front on paper that was due for shipment within two weeks of our operational start on July 1. Traditionally, we had gotten terms. "Welcome to the real world," said one of my small-business friends.

What surprises and problems should managers-turned-owners expect and prepare for? Lots, said our buyout managers.

"Market downside," answered Vaughn L. Beals, chairman/CEO of Harley-Davidson Motor Co.

"Self-complacency," answered the chairman/CEO of another firm employing 2,300, who asked to remain unidentified.

"The one danger of going private is that exclusive of your lender, you're really not answerable to anyone," said Jerry Gura.

Freedom and independence in your new business buyout will have their costs. You will be faced with new responsibilities and risks. There will be fewer controls on you, your life, and business.

But you will have fewer controls you can use in areas outside of your business. Pulling away from the parent corporation will disrupt your information sources and early-warning systems. You will need to replace them immediately.

You will need to create new communications and management systems — systems for following your decisions and policies through to implementation.

You will find new ways to interact continuously with outsiders such as consultants, customers, suppliers, your peers in the industry, and, of course, your counselors and members of your board of directors.

Gura said, "We know some people who tend to let their guard down. They are reveling in their glory. But our business, retailing, is very unforgiving. Once you goof, you goof, and it is very costly. We need to keep each other sharp."

We faced another early crisis with one of our key printers after our buyout of Garden Way Publishing. The printer said the terms we were expecting only applied to the parent company. He told us we would have to work with a reduced credit limit (and we were already well beyond that) before they could be comfortable with our new company and give us the old terms. This news meant we had to instantly develop alternative suppliers who were happy to work with us. Significantly, we are better balanced today in terms of printing and paper suppliers than we've ever been.

Many Surprises

You will be faced with similar surprises every day. Some will be good, some bad. The response to your buyout by employees will be a surprise — not exactly what you anticipated. The inventory you inherit will include some surprises. The accounts payables will contain some surprises.

Mail clerks at the parent company or in your local post office may be returning mail orders not addressed to their satisfaction. A long-time customer may use the occasion of the buyout to desert you for a competitor. A trusted assistant who seemed to share your vision of an independent company decides to remain with the parent corporation.

Our advice: don't take any of those changes personally. One of our directors said, "You've got to come back like a punching bag every hour when you're on your own." And remember, there's always another supplier, customer, and employee. Fight like hell to keep the good ones you have, but don't cry over those you lose.

In your new independent business, you will miss those corporate cushions you had, such as the corporate funds. To yourself, you can blame unexpected business problems on the recession, on the election, or on the weather, but you will have to pay for their costs out of your own pocket.

The timing of your buyout may have been perfect for the seller and the lender, but it may turn out to be all wrong for your employees or customers.

Your role as an entrepreneur will be to expect and welcome the surprises as a continuing flow of opportunities to learn, correct, and improve. There will be no more running to headquarters for shelter.

New Competition

Larry Munini said he faced unexpected hazards in the marketplace after his purchase of Genesys Software Systems. Instead of two major competitors, Munini found four.

Tom Madsen, who led the Key Technology buyout from Applied Magnetics, told a similar story of more scrutiny from both suppliers and customers.

"Our customers range from large to small food processors, but we do business with all the large food companies — Campbell's Soups, General Foods — and these companies sometimes feel one way about doing business with a company that is backed by an Applied Magnetics and they feel another way when all of a sudden there is a management buyout.

"You have to convince them. In a couple of cases we had to demonstrate to our customers that we had staying ability, because we are talking big-ticket items.

"Luckily, we had a long track record on a personal basis with these customers. There was credibility there. Had we been with the company only two years before we bought it, I think that could have been a much tougher problem."

It Gets Lonely

Executives-turned-entrepreneurs are also surprised, according to the *Harvard Business Review,* by "a pervading sense of loneliness." [2]

In a survey of 300 small-business CEOs, the *HBR* reported a high correlation between loneliness and stress in 109 respondents who complained of frequent loneliness: "Among respondents to our survey, 68 percent reported they had no confidant with whom they could share their deep concerns."

The truth of the matter is that you frequently look over your shoulder and find there is no one there for support anymore. I remedy this by making phone calls every day to sales reps, distributors, potential customers, and suppliers. You'll wonder where the time went.

After doing its survey of loneliness among small-business owners, the *Harvard Business Review* presented several recommendations for curing this. Among them:

● Participate in organizations of business leaders.
● Be attentive to family, friends, customers, and suppliers, and seek their counsel.
● Look for recreational and social activities that balance job-related isolation such as team sports and other group activities.

Sources of Support

Your most important source of support and outside information, of course, will be your outside professional counselors. That's what they're getting paid for.

Think of your counselors as your silent business partners, and keep them as well informed as the insiders.

Continually ask your counselors questions — all the right questions. Listen carefully to their answers.

Previously, in your management career, you were sheltered from certain economic realities by the parent corporation. Now you need to learn how to make your own forecasts and cope with business uncertainties.

Keep notes of conversations with your counselors and advisors. Then make a rough copy of those notes and send it back to them for their hand-written observations. You may find you missed some hints and offhand remarks that were intended to be danger signals.

Retain only the counselors and advisors who share your enthusiasm and will tell you what you can do as well as what you cannot do. Seek alternatives with them through a continuing dialogue.

If you've completed your buyout with an advisor who continues to remain withdrawn and uncommunicative, arrange for a timely switch to a more responsive professional.

Supports Missed

Buyout managers frequently reported they were surprised how much they missed corporate supports such as accounting and computer services.

"We thought it would be great to get rid of the corporate charge on our profit and loss statements for which we didn't think we really got much," Tom Madsen said with a laugh. "But we found out there are a lot of other charges that crop up [to replace the missing corporate services]."

Visit your advisors at their offices and ask for a full inventory of all available services. Establish a line of communications with all of their assistants.

Devise a process for keeping your lenders informed and protected from your surprises. Talk with them about new products, new customers, and new problems. Include them in your discussions of long-range financial planning. Ask them to keep you posted on available industry and government marketing research.

In my own case, I found myself, the entrepreneur, taking fifty trips in the first year of business. In my last year as a senior executive at Garden Way, Inc., I made half that number.

Be sure your outside accountants understand that their work for you must go beyond tax returns and financial reviews. Keep them involved in overall reviews of your inside financial operations, from petty cash to raising capital. Ask them to help with planning for employee benefits, insurance, profit centers, and internal controls.

Taking a business away from a parent company and setting up your own shop is like starting a new family in a new home. How your business grows and develops, just as your family does, will include some surprises.

Your Changing Relationships

"Some of the surprises are the way you're viewed by employees and fellow workers," according to Lou Auletta of Bauer/Electro.

"My true role is not that much different. I have retained my role as general manager. But, all of a sudden, as an owner, people looked at me differently. You are tested a lot more."

Auletta said the changes in business relationships, although exhilarating, can be inhibiting "to a degree."

Larry Munini of Genesys Software said he was first uneasy at first with his high visibility as company president. He said he sometimes still feels uncomfortable when his salespeople portray him publicly as a "bigger than life" problem-solver and force him to go out and live up to that image.

Employees Apprehensive

Tom Madsen said his Key Technology employees at first felt some apprehension about his insider buyout from Applied Magnetics with three other top managers.

"This was not malicious. The same thing happened when the firm was first acquired by Applied Magnetics in 1968. Up to that time, the company had been privately owned. The employees became apprehensive and formed a union. This was voted out three years later.

"Being aware of that previous experience, we did our very best job at communications," Madsen said. "We have about one hundred and forty people in our company, and I can get them all in one room and talk. We did that. We also had small group meetings about changes in benefit plans — how the new plans were going to be structured. We basically kept the plans just the way they had been.

"We wanted the employees to view it as much as possible as a continuation of business as usual," Madsen said.

"There are seven people on the management staff. Four of them became owners....The people who got involved had all expressed an interest in wanting to do this. But it was tough trying to decide. We operate pretty much as a group. All of them are still here. That was a tough decision — who should [participate in the buyout] and who shouldn't."

Changes in Attitude

Dick Hug of Environmental Elements said, "The attitude and productivity change is amazing. It is probably not unlike most other LBOs.

"We did it through a lot of sessions. Big sessions. Small group sessions. One-on-one sessions. I involved myself personally in almost all of the sessions to explain what we had done, why we had done it, what effect it would have on our people, and what kind of rewards they could expect if we were successful.

"Basically, we told them how good the company is, the kind of reputation we have in the marketplace, and the kind of pride that they could have in the company," Hug said.

"We have to work on it continually. We share our financials with almost everybody in the company. We don't have any secrets to speak of, but we expect them to keep that information confidential and not to be talking to their friends, neighbors, or the newspapers....They have a sense of involvement in knowing what's going on. I think that's important, to bring people into the fold.

"We have five hundred and eleven employees. They understand what we are doing and are better motivated with a better sense of purpose.

"It becomes infectious. We literally have five hundred and eleven people in this company who are cheerleaders."

Hug said that since the sale, relations between Environmental Elements and Koppers have remained good. "I have been with the company [Koppers] for a long time, and I have a lot of friends with the company. Most everyone in the company was really for me. Although there are always some jealousies that develop in a thing of this nature — someone wonders, 'Why didn't I do it?'— for the most part the relationships have been good."

At Storey Communications, we launched a weekly meeting for all ten employees, then a monthly meeting when we reached twenty. Now, at thirty, we meet on a staffwide basis each quarter, and communications are considered good.

Relationship with Customers

Regarding relationship changes with customers. Auletta said, "I felt comfortable in taking over the business because I had a good rapport with the customers and a good understanding of what they were looking for.

"The customers realize they are dealing with the president and the owner of the company, and I think that is very positive. They know that you will back up any commitment you make. This is very important."

Regarding his business relationship with his partner, Doug Baker said, "While I was a virtual optimist, my partner was a bit more conservative. We balance ourselves very well. I have the drive. He has the reins.

"I admit to myself I could have overstepped on several occasions, but he knew when to pull in," Baker said of his partner.

Family Relationships

Your buyout could also mean profound changes in your family relationships. In many of the buyouts we researched, wives, sons, and daughters are now working in the business and making the buyout a family affair.

Dick Hug's son joined him at Environmental Elements. Lou Auletta's son is with him at Bauer/Electro.

Dick Snyder of Snyder General Corporation has been married twenty six years and has three grown children in or recently graduated from college. "My wife is very actively involved in the business now in advertising and sales promotions," Snyder said. "It's really brought the family close together," he said of his buyout. "The business is a huge part of our life. All the kids want to know what's going on."

In doing research for this book, we called a Connecticut firm and asked to speak to the CEO. Let's call him Mr. Oliver. He was out of the office and his secretary was away from her desk, the telephone operator said. She asked, "May I help you?"

We took a chance and explained our hope of interviewing Mr. Oliver for this book. We were well aware that many "telephone operators" are in reality management assistants skilled at shielding the boss from salesmen, local politicians, news reporters, book authors, and other interruptions.

"Mr. Oliver is usually very interested and cooperative with this type of thing. I'll tell him you called, and he will probably be glad to meet with you....This is Mrs. Oliver."

Everyone Works

Or take our own case. On any Sunday afternoon, our eighteen-year-old daughter can be found finishing a filing project. Our fifteen-year-old mows the lawns, and our ten-year-old empties the wastebaskets. Martha Storey, a company officer and a full-time company production manager, handles everything from paper purchases to conference-room cleanups. As she stopped in our meeting room recently to say goodbye, she reminded, "Don't forget to take out the trash, John."

It's difficult to find families more involved in the business than at Doug Baker's restaurant and motor inn business in Vermont. Baker's partnership is with his wife's brother, Jim Kendall, and their two wives. The two families and their parents have homes adjacent to the business and their children have all worked in the business.

"Try to maintain a balance between your family life and your business life," Baker said. "The family is going to have to learn to give up a little. But you've got to learn when to leave the business at the office and go home and be with your family.

"Too often, when you shift gears going into a buyout, you let the business dominate you, and soon you have a family situation which can overlap into the business. Then you've got a real problem."

Baker said working closely and intently with a spouse in the business is a matter of having the right attitude. "Each of you is intelligent and brings something that the other doesn't have. Each of you has an instinct for a certain portion of the business. She knows certain areas. You know certain areas. And you have to accommodate each other in that way.

"It takes some adjustment. It doesn't come overnight. It comes over a period of time. It's a learned experience.

"It's a partnership....Many businesses have failed where the husband and wife tried to work together and failed simply because one or both have been unbending. And you both get burned....I would call that an inbred inability to accept the other as a partner."

Managing As An Entrepreneur

Do you believe effective management is accomplished only under tension applied from above?

Or are you more comfortable relaxing the rules and fostering a team effort in an entrepreneurial environment?

The style in which you organize and manage your new firm is too important to be left to charisma, chance, or management systems carried over from the parent corporation.

Keep yourself sensitive to the reasons you decided to embark on your insider buyout. Don't assume your employees will be as enthusiastic about the deal as you are. A frightened and insecure work-force could cause you trouble while you are busy launching your new firm.

In the absence of parent-company support systems, you will need to stop and think carefully. Who is supposed to do what, when, where, to whom, and how much it will cost?

You will need to foster an environment for developing your own new business culture. And, as your business grows, you will need to encourage adjustments to suit, not stunt, your dynamic new situation.

Our own goals are simple, to build supportive, communicative relationships with our employees, and perhaps long-standing relationships with our customers.

Employees will follow the rules, use the controls, and meet the goals you ask them to help you write. Fit the organization to the expertise of your employees, not the other way around.

Attitude Toward Money

Dick Hug of Environmental Elements said, "Our biggest challenge was changing the mentality of the work force. They are no longer working for a large company where a few extra dollars here and a few extra dollars there don't count. They no longer spend money quite as freely and as loosely as they did in the past. Not that the business was managed loosely before, but it's just a different mentality. We had to reinforce that among our people.

"We cut our salaried employment about 20 percent. Most of those people took early retirement. Many had lost their drive and mission in life. We worked out a good severance plan with Koppers as part of our buyout deal. Then we renegotiated the pension and health-medical plans to effect phenomenonal savings," Hug said.

Communications

Your first step in a dynamic business reorganization is to establish interactive, as opposed to hierarchical, systems for communications and meetings.

This process will permit a gradual evolution of your management systems, systems you will design and implement as you progress together with those employees involved.

Put your best efforts into teaching, leading, and encouraging your employees as opposed to directing, supervising, and controlling them. Teach them to be self-starting and self-managing. Instill pride through recognition and rewards for their commitment and innovation.

We made a lot of changes in our first month, moving corporate offices 125 miles, moving 300,000 books to Harper & Row in Scranton, Pennsylvania, hiring ten new persons, and reducing overhead by $500,000. We could not have done it without a committed new staff who shared our vision.

Training Employees

Executives today are benefiting from "transforming leadership" — techniques that concentrate on training employees, as opposed to "transactional leadership" — techniques that merely outline a quid pro quo employment transaction: this according to consulting psychologist Mortimer R. Feinberg and management professor Aaron Levenstein. [3]

Writing in the *Wall Street Journal* on dynamic leadership techniques, Feinberg and Levenstein cited six imperatives of successful executives:

1. Show a personal interest in individual progress.

2. Build charismatic relationships.

3. Encourage other people to shine.

4. Provide psychological support.

5. Ask questions, in a special, probing way.

6. Keep people informed.

If organizational problems persist in your new business, don't try to wing it with management solutions left over from the '60s or '70s. Seek state-of-the-art help from consultants who are expert in "organization development," a discipline that has evolved from the studies of management and human relations.

Managing Money

After your insider buyout, you will be managing more than people. You will also be managing capital.

Managing capital means projecting your capital needs, organizing and securing the financing, appropriating the funds, directing and controlling the spending, and accounting for all of these activities.

As a division manager, you were held accountable for the profitability of your division, but you had the parent company behind you to share the blame and losses during poor years.

As a manager-owner, you will not have this backup. You need to follow even more closely your costs of sales and production down to the bottom line.

You cannot avoid the fact that you as an individual are totally responsible for the payroll.

Lou Auletta of Bauer/Electro said, "Before, I always did a good job at making the company profitable for the owners. But I was amazed at how differently you look at things as the owner. You have a different set of eyes when you become the owner. You are much more conscious of things that you took for granted before, such as employee benefits.

"I have looked at this as an opportunity to do better for the employees as well as management," Auletta said.

Looking Ahead

Look for mistakes and misjudgments in your deal and don't be afraid to admit you made your share. Make your corrections immediately.

You will need to revise continuously your plans and goals, especially from your changing perspectives as a new owner-manager.

The company reorganization that will follow your buyout will be the time for you to stop doing what you were doing and start heading where you want to go.

Reorganize your new company into profit centers, each with its own budget and performance goals. Establish at the beginning a divestment policy that will weed out the losers.

Study each of your new policies and decisions for the impact upon your employees and resources.

Seize this opportunity to apply new productivity measurements to goals, not to activities. Fine tune your systems for estimating costs, sales, and production.

Institute new reporting systems for your sales, production, financials, and, most important, cash flow.

Implement controls for cash, expenses, accounts receivable, inventory, and, most of all, payroll.

"You try to go faster and further than your cash flow and your ability to earn will take you," Doug Baker said.

John W. Jordan of The Jordan Company said, "We always find the asset management companies improve dramatically. Once the guy's got his own money on the line he really doesn't need that extra half a million in inventory. And he's not about to let the customers take forty or fifty days to pay. And instead of paying his suppliers in fifteen days, he starts paying them in thirty-five days.

"You start to get a whole new dynamic and culture. That is, 'Save the buck. Start putting in the screws.' That is always good. It creates dollars on the bottom line. It's a dynamic resulting from a whole multitude of things," Jordan said.

When your division was with the parent corporation, you could ignore tax consequences and trust that the corporate staff counsel and accountants would solve the problems. Now you have to hire, educate, and supervise your own tax and accounting assistance, no matter whether this is in-house or out.

When You Need Money

Speaking of lenders, Tom Madsen said, "I heard this story before, and it is typical of what happened to us. After you buy the company, your bankers are your friends until you need them. During the first year or so of our operations, we were generating a fair amount of cash and the bankers were asking us, 'When are you going to borrow some money?'

"Then we went through about six months that were quite lean, with an order rate that was very low, and this drained our cash.

"We finally got to the point where we needed working capital, and, of course, at that point our receivables were quite low.

"Our business tends to be a seasonal business. This is not as much of a concern to us as it is to someone looking at the current P&L.

"When we went to the bank we found the cupboard rather bare....Our account is handled mainly through the Portland office.

"The local banker was very instrumental in helping us with the corporate bankers. He knew our business better, even though we had never had any previous banking relationships with him...He went to bat for us on the corporate level in Portland, and we were finally successful in extending our line of credit.

"And since that time they have traveled out here and now understand our business a lot better. I don't envision any further problems.

"You need to nurture those relationships, even when you don't need them. We don't need them now, but we're continuing to nurture them and educate the bankers as to where our company is going and where the industry is going. We have invited them to our trade shows and that sort of thing, so they really understand our business. Make them a partner with you so when you need them, they will be there."

For example, ask your lenders and other counselors to review and comment on your insurance coverage and your contingency plans. Plan ahead for quick financing response to technological or environmental demands.

Ask your lenders to keep you alerted to the latest problems and opportunities of the money markets and the national economy as they relate to your company financing.

Most important, in an insider buyout, focus on your cash flow, capital accounts, and reducing your debt. Less important now are profit-and-loss statements and quarterly earnings reports.

"Profits are for public companies," said Robert E. Lee, a partner in Maul Technology Corp., a $30 million 1981 buyout.

"As far as I'm concerned," Lee said, "profits are a cash drain because you pay half to Uncle.

"Cash flow is the lifeblood of any privately owned business."

In my case, I stopped looking for a monthly P&L statement and began looking at daily receipts and disbursements. What a difference a day makes.

Growing as an Entrepreneur

You have bought the company or division that you worked for. You have discovered how to get control of your business life. You have learned that freedom and independence are the thrills of a lifetime.

Now you need to be sure that in the rush to establish your new independent business, you are continuously making the right business decisions.

"You've got to face the fact that the buck stops here," Victor Kiam said.

"The manager in a large corporation can bluster and bluff, 'If I were making the decisions, this is what I'd do,'" Kiam said.

"But when he runs his own ship and it is his decision, the confidence he gained by presenting his ideas to a corporate group who then made the decision is shaken because he doesn't have that corporate group to go to.

"He sits in a little mental cubbyhole of his own, and he has to come up with the solution. Maybe he has some good people around him who will suggest what has to be done. But ultimately it is his decision."

Victor Kiam was talking about the loneliness of being both boss and owner, the difficulty of a corporate manager making the transformation from a player in the middle to the star at the top.

"Sometimes you cannot come up with a decision based on your intellect, and you have to come up with a decision based on your feelings, on emotion. Your gut is what's going to tell you what's right or wrong.

"And once you've done it, you cannot let on that you may have misgivings. You have a whole group of people who are dependent on you and your decision. You've got to bull it through. You've got to keep going. You cannot show your doubts."

As a corporate manager, you were trained to make decisions. But as an owner-manager, Kiam said, you must go beyond the mere making of decisions into an expanded role of championing your decisions.

"You've got to exude confidence that you're sure of your decisions. Don't sit on a decision for three months. Make the decisions and make them decisively.

"I've always felt that making no decision is worse than making a poor decision. Be decisive once you get in there."

Kiam, a veteran at business buyouts, is not suggesting that owner-managers make their decisions decisively in lonely isolation after consulting only their gut reactions.

Choosing a Board

Kiam believes you should beef up your board of directors with strong personalities who will ride herd on you.

"When I went into my first business deal, about 1967, I tried to get people around me that other people would respect, so that I would be known by the company that I kept. I didn't get personal friends I could maneuver....A lot of public companies have rubber stamp boards.

"I went out and got the most difficult, the most honorable people who were proven successes so that no one could say Kiam had a mamby-pamby group that was a rubber stamp."

A strong board of directors as recommended by Kiam is not a threat to your life's goals of business control and personal independence. A strong board of directors is a challenge to your intellect, and it can strengthen your business and ensure that you reach your life's goals.

In an insider buyout, your board of directors does not hire you, you hire its members. The relationship is similar to the one you have with your lawyer and accountant. If you ignore their advice, you don't get fired. They withdraw and go spend their efforts and expertise where they are better utilized and respected.

At Storey Communications, we're blessed with a strong board of directors. Professionals all, from New York, Boston, and Connecticut, they travel quarterly for no compensation. At a recent meeting, Martha gave them each a basket of Vermont cheese. Don stood up and said, "You guys have given us millions of dollars' worth of advice, all for a piece of cheese. Thanks." The fact is, we couldn't have afforded their advice, and they weren't asking to get paid.

Board Members

The people you need on your board are your outside peers or mentors. They are people with expertise that balances or exceeds your experience, people who can serve as your confidants and counselors in a close professional and personal relationship.

Select board members for professional reasons, not as a payoff for services rendered or anticipated, and certainly not for any perceived public-relations benefits.

"Board of directors" is the accepted term, but if you are worried about losing control of your business before you've had time to enjoy it, think of your board of directors as an advisory board or council of advisors.

"I'm the sole owner [of Remington Products] and the company is very successful," Kiam said. "But if you attended our board meetings, you'd think these guys each had an equivalent stake in the business and that the company is...about to go bankrupt. It's that kind of a knock-down, drag-out meeting.

"On my board, when we started out, I had a financial guy, a former managing partner of a major accounting firm, and my personal lawyer.

"When we went into the retail business with a chain of special retail stores, I added a very astute retailer because I didn't know retailing. My retail operating manager would come to me, and I couldn't really help him when he needed help. So we asked this gentleman to go on our board, and they [the veteran retailer and the operating manager] now have a one-on-one relationship.

"And I have just added a senior marketing chap because I was the only marketing guy on the board. So when I talked about a marketing idea...they said that was a lousy idea because of the legal, tax, or accounting implications. But they didn't look at it from the marketing point of view. I added a guy for marketing so they would have the benefit of someone else's input...so if I came up with something they though was a hairbrainer...there was another voice.

"You want people who are going to argue with you," Kiam said. "If you try to get a mirror image of yourself, a yes man, so that you can live a happy, contented life with no discussions and arguments, you're going to be a failure.

"You want people who have strong opinions, who are able, who are going to argue like hell with you so that you have to prove your point.

"It's very key," Kiam said. "When you're out on a limb, you've got to get the best brains you can get."

Many Participate

At Unitog, Bob Hagans said twenty-nine employees are shareholders, and there is a "great desire to have every employee" a part-owner.

"It has changed the attitude. These are not sophisticated investors. Now they have second mortgages on their homes. Our good managers have become great managers.

"Everything we've got, we've got in it. All our physical and monetary resources. And our first year has been super."

Worth the Gamble

"It was more than worth the gamble," Jerry Gura said. "I had nothing to lose. I could have always stepped back to a corporate job."

"If something did not work out," Tom Madsen said, " well, we just never thought about what would happen if things did not work out. Except that we are all young enough so that we could go out again and do our own things."

Dick Hug said, "A lot of people ask, after twenty-six years of working for a major company, going up through the ranks, and doing relatively well, 'Why would you think of becoming an entrepreneur?'

"I think it's a tremendous way to go. There are some tremendous opportunities out there for those who are willing to take a little bit of risk."

Hug said he was inspired to do his insider buyout by entrepreneurial friends in the 4,000-member Young Presidents' Organization, an association of chief executive officers under the age of fifty who attained their positions before the age of forty.

"I got to thinking, 'If they can do it, by golly, I can do it.'

"I gave a talk with my partner to a group of persons on what we had done, and they were all amazed at how we had leveraged and structured it. I ended that talk by saying, 'If I can get one of you to do an LBO over the next twelve months, I'll feel the time was well spent."

"The most important thing I hope we can get out of this book is to get one other person to do it," Hug said.

Victor Kiam said the rules for performing a small buyout are the same as those for doing the bigger deals.

"All the points we have touched upon [in this book] existed in my situation as well.

"Whether you do a $1 million, a $10 million, a $200 million, or even a $200,000 deal, you still need all the basic guidelines we have discussed.

"And you certainly need the support and guidance of other people who are much more steeped in certain other areas than you are," Kiam said.

Proud of Buyout

"It's something that we're proud of," Lou Auletta said of his insider buyout." Anyone who's faced with a similar situation, I'm sure a few tips wouldn't hurt. This is an opportunity to share some of our experiences, having gone through it."

"There are going to be continuing [insider] acquisitions going on," Jerry Gura said. "Maybe to a greater degree than what we've witnessed — and we've certainly gone through some halcyon years. The most important thing from my perspective is SOS — the self-ownership-syndrome. That's where it's at."

Celebrating the Victory

When we completed our buyout of Garden Way Publishing, I was determined to rest, to savor the moment of success, to share that good feeling with my family and my friends. I wanted to go over with Don the many negotiating sessions, the days and nights of planning, our little victories and our defeats, much as athletes go over the big game.

Where was the best place to do this? The Virgin Islands? South Carolina?

And I planned to do this. I counted on it. But first there was the matter of finding a new home for the business, moving a huge inventory of books. I had to put off the victory celebration — just until next month.

And then there were the accounts receivable to handle, the new books to be created, the need to hold fast to old customers and to find new ones.

And more months slipped quickly past.

Now two years have gone by, busy years, years of growth. And it's certainly much too late to think of a victory celebration.

Maybe we've had that celebration already, in odd moments, on the phone with Don, at breakfast with Martha, in quick conversations with many others who, like us, tried an insider buyout and found it one of the most satisfying experiences of their business careers.

And just perhaps the writing of this book has been part of that celebration. For this book has given us an opportunity to share with you and other readers the thrills of that buyout.

And we sincerely hope that it gives you the push you need to try an insider buyout of your own.

If you're the entrepreneurial type, wanting to try it on your own in the business world, we can assure you that you'll never work harder in your life, never get so scared about business matters, never put yourself to a sterner test — and never feel more sure of yourself, more elated than when you try your own insider buyout and it works.

Chapter X References:

[1] "Going It Alone," by Robert Johnson, *The Wall Street Journal,* February 6, 1985.

[2] "Growing Concerns: The Loneliness of the Small-Business Owner," David E. Gumpert and David P. Boyd, *The Harvard Business Review,* November-December 1984.

[3] "Transforming Your Employees Through Dynamic Leadership," by Mortimer R. Feinberg and Aaron Levenstein, *The Wall Street Journal,* 1984.

Chapter XI

How Others Did It

In our extensive interviews with corporate leaders who were involved in buyouts, we found their stories had much to teach us about the wide variety of circumstances and methods that can be involved in these buyouts.

We noted, too, that all of these had one thing in common. They involved people who saw opportunity where others might see a threat, people who not only saw the opportunity but seized it.

Just how they did this is explained in the following pages.

Genesys Software Systems, Inc.

Providing complete employee accounting and personnel management information systems for Fortune 500 companies and top commercial banks is the business niche of the four-year-old Genesys Software Systems of Lawrence, Massachusetts.

Genesys designs customized software that provides clients with nationwide, terminal-to-terminal access and analysis of employee records from the first job application on through the final retirement benefit.

Genesys was created out of Lawrence J.Munini's $5 million insider buyout of a Wang Laboratories' software department in 1981. It was an obvious divestiture: the software is programmed for IBM mainframes while Wang's main mission is manufacturing computer hardware in competition with IBM.

Munini's story is a classic case of how a trusted manager with little capital, no acquisition experience, and a short timetable buys the division he loves from a benevolent parent corporation.

Munini hocked everything he owned and could get among friends, fellow managers, and venture capital contacts to raise the $500,000 down payment.

But the Genesys management group retained 51 percent equity in the new company and has paid off Wang. Sixteen Wang employees moved with Munini to Genesys, which now employs nearly 100 people.

"We organized ourselves to be a big company in big company style — even when we were just starting," Munini said. "Now we are starting to grow into that. The people who came along are now in senior positions — vice presidents."

His advice on financing: "Don't let financing stand in your way. There's tons of money out there.

"After I handed in my first proposal, I decided I needed some financial backing. I went home that night, whipped out a sheet of paper, and wrote down the names of everybody I had business contacts with. Then I started hitting the phone, dialing.

"The first gentleman I dialed used to be the vice president of Wang. I had been reporting to him, so I had a good working relationship with him.

"I said, 'Hello, guess what? I'm buying the software package and I'm looking for backing. Do you want to contribute?' He said, 'Sure, count me in for $100,000.' I said, 'Great,' hung up and said, 'Hey, this is going to be a piece of cake. I'm looking for six or seven hundred thousand and the first guy throws in one hundred.'

"Then I called my neighbor, who put me in touch with my attorney. He also put me in touch with a private investor, let's call him Old Charlie, who had bought and sold a couple of computer companies in the Boston area....I went down and gave him my spiel. Sure, no sweat, $400,000, and he starts giving me all sorts of advice about how to negotiate with Dr. Wang.

"I figured I was over the hump. I figured the employees who went with me would pick up another $100,000 and we'd be all set.

"The deal was going to happen by June 30 [1981] because...they wanted to take the profits of the sale on the current fiscal year. This was the week before Memorial Day in late May. The attorney for Wang legal department walked into my office and said, 'Here, sign this.... You're the official winner of the bid, and we're putting you on paid leave of absence until June 30 when the deal will be signed. We want you to get out of the building because we don't want anybody to claim that there's any kind of conspiracy or chicanery here. You're going to set up this new company and we don't want anybody to accuse anybody of anything. We're going to put you out on the street at full salary. Go set up a company and get busy.'

"So, basically, I did. I started scrambling. I got a real deal on a building. We bought some desks and chairs. It became early June, then middle June, and June 30 was coming when I had to put down a half a million for the down payment. I went to buddy Old Charlie, and said, 'How about the money?'

"Charlie said, 'Well, we've got to write an agreement. We've got to do this, and we've got to do that, and we've got to have assurances of this, and you've got to cover this liability and that liability,' and I said, 'What? What do you want all these assurances for? Nobody's giving me any assurances.'

"We had a couple of very unsatisfactory conversations and about a week before June 30, he upped the ante, which amounted to me throwing in my first-born son or something like that. I told him I wasn't interested in that. He said, 'You've got to agree or the deal is off.' I said, 'I guess the deal is off.'

"I walked out, and said, "Hmmmm. This is your basic tight jam. How am I going to cough up $500,000 in ten days?"

"I called Dr. Wang, made an appointment, walked in, and said, 'Gee, I have some bad news. My arrangement with Charlie is off, and it will take me a little longer to line up some financial backing.'

"So Dr. Wang gave the word, and the lawyers got busy and reworked the agreements so I had another ninety days to arrange long-term financing."

For the down payment, Munini "pulled a half a million dollars out of a hat" with short-term borrowing on everything he owned. He signed the papers on June 30, moved into new quarters, and launched his business on schedule — thanks to the ninety days granted by Dr. Wang to continue his hunt for long-term financing.

"I was out there running the company with ninety days to scramble around [for long-term financing]. There is this class of stock brokers — I call them professional Wang watchers. One of them called me and said, 'I know all the bigwigs at Wang and I heard you had just spun out and need some money.' At that time I had a couple of other flakey things going, so I said, 'Thanks, but no thanks,' but I took his name and number and was off chasing some other things.

"About two weeks later those things had fallen through the cracks, so I called this guy back. He came over to check us out to see if we were real. He introduced me to a venture capitalist who was familiar with the software industry and understood that we had comparatively few hard assets on the books.

"By coincidence, in September we have an annual trade show of all our customers. These are people from big companies who had recieved a notice that Wang had sold the product. So a crowd of 500 buyers showed up to see if these new guys were going to cut it or whether they should go back and recommend to their managers to buy another software package. It was an important event for us.

"The venture capitalist said, 'I'll come along. If I like what your customers say, I'll put my money in.' He wandered around the convention floor and came to the conclusion that these were all big companies and they had their whole data processing and payroll operations dependent on our software package and they weren't going to go away. He said, 'Sure, I'm in,' and that represents about 22 percent of the equity."

Cherry Webb & Touraine (CWT)

This group of fifty women's specialty stores headquartered in South Attleboro, Massachusetts, was bought in November, 1982, from the Outlet Company of Providence, Rhode Island, by President Gerald A. Gura and three other top managers.

Jerry Gura said, "It was an eighteen-month ordeal which ranged from Houston to Boston. We traveled the nation. We went to twenty-six venture capitalists, fourteen banks, and over a dozen private investors.

"The best way to learn is to go through the motions.

"Doing your homework is very important. Disclosure is very important.

"It is the nature of banks to demand considerably more in security than the amount they are lending you.

"The most important thing you can bring to the table is a comprehensive history of the company, a clear-cut characterization of what has been accomplished, detailed five-year pro formas with cash flows — and integrity.

"My prospectus [business plan] was about fifty to sixty pages.

"What we attempted to do was to clarify who we were, capsulize the history, with the best explanations of why certain things occurred, both good and bad, and hype the explanations of the pro forma assumptions.

"But there should also be conservatism in this approach. It shouldn't be pie in the sky.

"Even those venture capitalists who expressed interest but then declined were talking about very little of their capital — but seventy-five to eighty percent of the ownership.

"Then we sought financing help from an oil man who led us to the Penn Square Bank. In consideration of this, plus a small amount of cash, the oil man was going to be fifty percent partner.

"We negotiated a loan with the Penn Square Bank, but two weeks before we were to draw our letter of credit, they went under. Then things began to get exciting.

"Our partner evidently thought he had us in a tight spot. He found some new lenders in St. Louis, but wanted to increase his stake to two-thirds. This was during a Sunday evening telephone call.

"Forgetting the principle that any part of the pie is better than none," Gura said he severed connections with the would-be partner at that moment.

"Then I went to Bruce Sundlem [president of CWT's parent company, the Outlet Company of Providence] and said, 'Look, I'm afraid if I get into bed with this individual, that he may attempt to rape the company, especially if he controls it. I don't want to sign my name to that kind of a situation.'

"Bruce was highly respectful, quite taken by the integrity, and said, 'Look, let me see what I can do to get the board to take back another $3.5 million.' He did and that made the deal for us with a subordinated note.

"This was all the more interesting because just prior to this, the board had sold ninety-one stores to a New Jersey company that had gone belly-up. Going back to the board of directors to help another group of undercapitalized people, I think was a really gutsy thing for Mr. Sundlem to do.

"With that financing in hand, we were able to get the asset-based lending division of the Chase Manhattan behind us and put the deal together.

"As it turned out, we retained one hundred percent of the ownership.

"We would have settled for any reasonable portion of the pie rather than nothing, if we had the right partner. We were just interested in gaining a share and then being the active management.

"The clincher was that, one, we were delivering results [for Outlet] and were not the same kind of management team that their previous sale had gone to. Two, I think they respected the fact that we had not prostituted ourselves. And, three, they respected the fact that a firm like Chase was also involved."

Since buying out the firm, the new owners-managers have paid off all of their debt to the Outlet Company — and did it nine years ahead of schedule.

"The only lender we have today is our bank and a small amount of long-term debt," Gura said.

Harley-Davidson Motor Co.

Harley-Davidson is the only surviving American motorcycle manufacturer. And many bike riders consider the Harley with its big, V-Twin engine the only surviving "real" motorcycle.

So when a white paper began circulating at AMF recommending divestiture of Harley-Davidson as a subsidiary, the managers were quick to act in saving the legendary "Hog" from any further indignities.

The June, 1981, insider buyout for $75 million by thirteen managers was 98 percent outside financed but left management with 100 percent of the equity. Vaughn L. Beals is chairman of the board and chief executive officer of this Milwaukee-based corporation.

Faced with stiff overseas competition but supported by its legions of loyal riders, the company turned to computer engineering for solutions to some historic technical problems while preserving the potency of its big-bike, easy-riding image.

Cycle magazine gave the buyout managers a welcome pat on the back: "The big twin has been brought up to date and yet it remains recognizably a Harley-Davidson engine — not a futuristic contrivance that would be instantly rejected as spurious by The Faithful. Harley is banking on the hope that it has now fulfilled its social contract and that The Faithful will now do their part."

Bauer/Electro Inc.

The official customer list of Bauer/Electro today reads like an international who's who in the aircraft and airline industry. The company in Farmington, Connecticut manufactures sophisticated testing equipment for aircraft engines and fuel systems.

In 1983, when Louis J. Auletta, Sr. heard Bauer Electro [as it was then named] would be sold, he had been with the company for eleven years, including six years as general manager.

To explore the possibility of an insider buyout, Auletta hired a two-man investment consulting firm, MacArthur/Nathan Associates of Springfield, Massachusetts.

When it became apparent Auletta needed more equity, he asked the consultants, John R. MacArthur and Larry R. Nathan, to join him as partners. The deal left Auletta with 66 percent of Bauer/Electro and his partners with 34 percent.

"We're looking at some fairly impressive growth potential over the next three to five years," Auletta said. "The aircraft industry has come out of some very tough times."

Founded in 1910 as Bauer & Company, an electrical contracting firm, the company at the time of the buyout was a subsidiary of Electro Methods of South Windsor, Connecticut, an aircraft parts manufacturer.

Bauer/Electro now employs about fifty people, of whom one-third are in engineering. The modern, 24,000-square-foot plant is in the beautiful Farmington Industrial Park. Working in a plant surrounded by woods, President Auletta frequently looks out the picture windows in his office to see deer wander by.

For Auletta, Bauer/Electro is not only a job, a career, and an investment, but it is also a family affair. His wife works several days a week as an administrative assistant and receptionist. And his son, a Lehigh University graduate with a degree in industrial engineeering, is the company's chief of manufacturing.

Environmental Elements

The recession led officials of Koppers Company, Inc. of Pittsburgh to target Environmental Elements Corporation of Baltimore for divestiture.

And it was his confidence in the future need for Environmental Elements's product line in air, sound, waste, and water pollution controls that led the subsidiary's president, Richard E. Hug, to organize an insider buyout.

Hug and nine other top managers bought 74 percent of the company in July, 1983. The balance of the equity in the company is owned by several outside associates.

"It's been the most exciting thing in my career of ten years as president," Hug said.

"A lot of problems were solved by the buyout. The economy obviously has a great effect on our business. We ride to some extent upon the capital-spending cycle, and the economy turned around almost to the day we bought the business.

"We've been out of the banks since ten days after the close," Hug says of his company's need for borrowing.

"We have a very strong cash position and can finance our own growth internally at the present time as long as it is not explosive.

"We want to grow very modestly in the next two or three years and reduce some of our leverage, but be sensible about the way we grow," Hug said.

Hug recalls that "this was a very complicated and highly leveraged deal.

"Immediately after I had asked Koppers for a handshake on the acceptance of the proposal, I said to myself, 'I don't want all my eggs in one basket as far as the financing is concerned.' I had heard too many stories about greed that is associated with investment bankers, etcetera, etcetera, and I never had any first-hand experience. But I wanted to protect myself, number one, and number two, see if I could get better financing."

At this time, Hug had a financing commitment from a New York City investment banking firm.

"So I went to the city of Baltimore. Over the years I had been pretty well connected with the city because I had been very involved in civic activities. I asked them for an industrial revenue bond of $10 million to purchase the company on the basis that I had made a purchase offer to Koppers and if my purchase offer were not accepted it could be sold to an outside firm who might run it as is or might decide to close part of the facility and move someplace else.

"Within a matter of three weeks [in December, 1982] I had the commitment from the city of Baltimore and the City Council for a $10 million industrial development bond in my name — that was very key. Now suddenly I had control of $10 million which was essentially half the purchase price of the company.

"I felt that I would not have needed it, but on the other hand that alternative funding was much more expensive.

"The New York investment banking firm knew about it, but they were not encouraging me to seek the ID bond. They indicated they would probably not use it. I continued to question them why, when there was probably four or five percent [interest rate] difference.

"Their explanation was, 'Well, you know, we eventually want to take this business public, and if we're involved with an industrial revenue bond, it will be more difficult.'

"I just couldn't see leaving four or five interest points just sitting there in a highly leveraged transaction.

"After a couple of months of negotiating, in mid-February, the investment banking firm began to have increasing conflict with us about the way the business ought to go....They wanted to bring in their own man to run a portion of our business, the manufacturing portion. I was opposed to that because we had a very competent and capable man who had been with the company for years who was very, very good. I just saw that the investment bank [officials] wanted to exert their influence and get a bigger portion of the equity than we had previously agreed to.

"In the meantime they had never formalized a shareholders' agreement with me even though we had numerous conversations and a handshake on what the equity split was going to be. Basically, they indicated if I did not accede to their wishes and bring in their manager to run a part of the operation, I could forget their backing the deal.

"I told them this was not the deal we had when we went into this and I'd go it alone — not being sure at that time that I could do it alone, but knowing I had the industrial revenue bond.

"In the meantime, I talked Koppers into taking back the balance of the debt...in preferred stock and subordinated debentures.

"Koppers was very upset that the investment banking firm was now out of the picture because the investment banking firm had given them a high degree of comfort. They finally came back after several weeks of soul-searching and said, 'We're not going to let you do that. You're going to have to bring in somebody else to give us some comfort.'

"I contacted a friend of mine here in Baltimore who is chairman of a local investment banking firm and large regional securities house....He consented to come in as a comfort factor [along with] his firm and two other outside investors I've known for a long time. They are external board members for me and they [collectively] have a total of 26 percent.

"Senior management has 74 percent.

"Our deal is very highly leveraged. Ten senior managers had $500,000 equity in an $18 to $19 million deal. We financed about 97 percent. We used the principle of OPM — other people's money — to the greatest extent possible.

"And I did it without the help of the New York investment firm.

"I think the key was that Koppers took back about half the debt in preferred stock. That was done to provide for an equity appearance on the balance sheet. The balance of the debt, $5 or so million, is subordinated debentures. We have a thirty-month grace period on both principal payments which are due in an eight-month period.

"One of my basic goals and strategies was to get fixed-rate financing for the entire duration. We did. The bank gave us a fixed rate on the purchase of the industrial-revenue bond. And the subordinated debentures and preferred stock owned by Koppers are essentially fixed. So a fixed-rate financing to us in such a highly leveraged situation was an absolute must.

"We were not going to be plagued by the vagaries of the interest market, which obviously can put you out of business. We are going to be masters of our own destiny and not have to worry about that."

The Jordan Company

Insider buyouts need a lot of help from outsiders. One of the outsiders who has been behind some of the most successful insider buyouts is investor John W. (Jay) Jordan, III, a managing partner of The Jordan Company, New York, New York.

"We're basically a private investment company,"Jordan explained. "We don't have clients. We buy and own companies. In almost all cases management owns a chunk averaging 25 percent and we own the rest. We encourage the entrepreneurial approach, but they're not our clients, they're our partners.

"If the terms were right, we would sell it back to them. There is nothing excluded in our deals. We are very flexible."

The Jordan Company owns substantial interest in more than twenty-five companies with aggregate sales of more than $2 billion.

Among the more notable insider buyouts The Jordan Company has supported is the $21 million insider buyout in 1982 by three top managers of the Piece Goods Shop in Winston-Salem, North Carolina. The managers contributed $100,000 and retain a 25 percent equity, and Jordan contributed $300,000 for a 75 percent stake.

Another Jordan partner is Bench Craft, Inc., a Blue Mountain, Mississippi, upholstered furniture manufacturer. The original deal as engineered by Jordan in 1982 saw four Bench Craft managers join with ten other partners to sell the company, then buy back 50 percent equity for a net gain of $9.5 million. Later the managers took the firm public, retaining a 30 percent interest valued at $13.5 million. In March, 1985, Jordan engineered a deal in which Bench Craft bought Cal-Style, a Compton, California, manufacturer of casual dining furniture.

Jordan said the biggest advantage of the insider buyouts he has participated in was the solution of problems that had not previously been identified as business problems.

Key Technology

When Applied Magnetics Corporation of Goleta, California, decided to sell Key Electro Sonic of Milton-Freewater, Oregon, a manufacturer of sophisticated food-processing equipment, financing help for an insider buyout by four managers came from a most unusual source — Harold R. Frank, chairman of the seller's board of directors.

But the deal would not have happened without the desire and capabilities of Key president Thomas C. Madsen and his three partners from management, who concluded the $3.5 million buyout in December, 1982.

Explaining why they felt confident to tackle the buyout, Madsen said, "All the decision-making about where this company was going, although on a review basis, was being made at the local management level [before the buyout]. We always said we were managing or trying to manage the company as if we owned it. So in terms of product direction and marketing, that has remained essentially identical to the plans we had when we were a part of Applied Magnetics."

Madsen, 37, has been with Key for thirteen years and has been president since 1980. He recently received the Innovator Award of the year from *Food Engineering* magazine.

One of Key Technology's latest products for the prepared foods industry is an automatic defect removal system that optically scans and removes defects from French fries.

Another is the Thermo Flo pressure-processor which may be used for cooking, blanching, tempering, rehydrating, and shucking different foods. This features a hydraulically powered drive system and solid state programmable controls.

Madsen said the food processing industry was hard-hit by the 1980-81 recession and only recently has begun to grow again.

"We couldn't count on the type of capital expansion projects that we had done in the 1970s," Madsen said. "Our plan is to develop equipment that can provide a fairly rapid payback for the processor. The key is whether we can continue to develop the technology that we had started with Applied Magnetics. We continue to invest quite heavily in research and development.

"It's always tough for managers who have not done a buyout before. You can read a lot about big deals that are structured with small amounts of equity from the managers and this leads many to go into their deals with too high expectations.

"In our particular situation, our deal is structured so that if we meet certain financial objectives, then the manager-owners can take more equity as time goes along. It's an earn-your-way-in type of deal. I personally think that's healthier for all parties."

Pullman Transportation Co., Inc.

The 1984 reorganization of Pullman Transportation was not technically an insider buyout or a leveraged buyout.

It was the spin-out of Pullman from The Signal Companies. Followed by the sale by Pullman of all rail car assets to Trinity Industries. Followed by the purchase by Pullman of all assets of Trailmobile Inc. and Aerospace Division of UOP Inc. from The Signal Companies. Followed by the reelection of the subsidiary's former president, Thomas M. Begel, as the new president of the new public company, Pullman Transportation Co., in Princton, N.J.

You could call it an insider spin-out.

Begel has management control of Pullman and is a major stockholder of the $30 million firm. But the ultimate control of Pullman is vested in stockholders.

However, the decisions facing Begel in his insider spin-out of Pullman were similar to those facing managers in insider buyouts and are included here for their many similarities and few contrasts.

"I encouraged the key people that I hired here to go out and buy a fairly substantial block of stock, so that we would look at this business as shareholders as opposed to looking at it as professional managers. I think this is a very healthy thing for the company," Begel said.

"And this is one of the healthy things about leveraged buyouts in general. You get a guy thinking like an owner instead of a professional, paid manager. Sometimes that creates a very different perspective in running the company."

Two new strategic thrusts at Pullman since the spin-out, Begel said, are "professional management and flexibility."

Begel said he has hired the best professional managers available as chief financial officer, general counsel, and chief executive officer.

The projected income for Pullman during its first year was $200 million, a target Begel expects to exceed by about 7 percent. Trailmobile, a 140-year-old firm, is a maker of truck trailers. Aerospace manufactures seats and galley equipment for aircraft.

Begel has already steered Pullman into its first acquisition, for $40 million in cash: the REDM Industries, Inc. of West Paterson, New Jersey, makers of electrical and electronic components for industry and the military.

Once Pullman's cash flow is established, Begel said the company will begin looking for more diversified acquisitions.

Pullman is headquartered on Nassau Street overlooking the Princeton University campus.

"The time constraints are still more than I'd like," Begel said of heading the Pullman spin-out in comparison to managing it when it was part of the corporate hierarchy.

"But this is a part of the world we love. We bought a lovely little farm outside of town. I don't think my wife and [thirteen-year-old] daughter have ever been happier.

"They know I'm having just about the best time I've ever had in my life. And that has a lot of side benefits. When you enjoy what you're doing, it creates a whole different family and business situation."

Remington Products

Victor K. Kiam II, Remington chairman, needs no introduction. He's the man in the striped bathrobe on television who says he was so impressed with the Remington electric shaver his wife bought him that he bought the company, in Bridgeport, Connecticut.

Victor Kiam's buyout of Remington was not an insider buyout. It was an out-and-out outsider buyout by a veteran acquisition artist. But his perspectives are included here like Jordan's and Begel's for their similarities and contrasts.

Since Kiam brought Remington from Sperry in 1979 for $25 million, he has doubled his work force, tripled its sales, increased productivity, and lowered prices. Kiam credits part of his success to profit-sharing and other participative management techniques.

Of all the managers interviewed for advice about how to perform an insider buyout, none is busier than Victor Kiam, yet none was more cooperative. He talked to us at length from his home on a Saturday just before leaving for a month's sales trip to the Orient.

Snyder General Corporation

"The typical management buyout transaction as proposed by the financial community is that the owner-manager gets 20 percent or less of the equity and the passive investors get 80 percent or more of the company.

"I wanted to change that," Richard W. Snyder said. "As it turned out, I initially obtained 83 percent of the corporation."

With only $100,000 in cash and $200,000 in a personal loan, Snyder bought the climate control division of the Singer Company in February, 1982, for $27.5 million at a time when the assets were valued at $55 million.

"Now I own it all," Snyder said. "I bought out all the other equity players." He is president of the Dallas-based firm.

Snyder General's original Climate Control line includes the Comfortmaker and Electro-Hydronic heating and cooling products and the Electromode line of electric heating and refrigeration equipment.

Snyder has now added to the line with three other acquisitions: Arco Comfort Products (furnaces, air conditioners, and heat pumps); Halstead & Mitchell (refrigeration and heat transfer equipment); and McQuay Inc. (heat-transfer products and metal castings).

If it were publicly held, Snyder General today would be ranked among the Fortune 500 companies.

Snyder said there is no thought at Snyder General about going public within ten or fifteen years: "If there were some other major opportunities that we wanted to explore, we could. But right now, we like being a privately held corporation."

Sugarhouse Motor Inn & Restaurant

Douglas J. Baker, with his brother-in-law and partner, James Kendall, and their wives, Mary Baker and Donna Kendall, purchased 100 percent ownership of Cole's Motel and Restaurant in Middlebury, Vermont in 1972 in a deal that was 100 percent financed. The Bakers and Kendalls paid $200,000 for the property which had quadrupled in value and now employs about forty-five people.

After attending college in Vermont, Baker worked for a grocery chain and an aircraft manufacturer in Connecticut before joining Kendall as an employee at the motel-restuarant business.

Over coffee with the owner, Kendall discovered that he wanted to sell the business because his wife was ill. Kendall immediately expressed an interest in buying in and asked Baker to join him as a way to lend stability to the deal.

By way of testing the buyout, the partners leased the property for one year with an option to buy. In their early days of managing the business, Baker worked off-season as a cottage parent at a nearby state school for troubled youths and Kendall worked part-time as a plumber.

The business is now a landmark hospitality and business-meeting center midway between Vermont's two largest cities, Burlington and Rutland. But the partners and their wives have not lost their hands-on control of the business. At a major dinner meeting, patrons expect to see Kendall in cook's whites in the kitchen, Baker serving coffee or mixing drinks, and the wives at the front desk or waiting on tables.

TICOR

During the insurance industry's cyclic squeeze in 1983, Southern Pacific Company decided to sell TICOR, the Los Angeles-based title insurance company it had owned since 1979.

"It was not a happy acquisition," President Winston V. (Bud) Morrow said of TICOR's days with Southern Pacific.

Morrow sat in on some early discussions with a TICOR suitor, then decided inside managers could present their own buyout proposal with a little help from their friends.

Morrow called upon his old friend and mentor, Harold S. Geneen, who engineered the $271 million buyout of TICOR, the nation's largest title insurance company. The buyers included Geneen; Morrow; TICOR's chairman, Rocco C. Siciliano; another private investor; and the financial arm of American Can Company.

Management retained about 11 percent of the equity in the October, 1983, reorganization.

Morrow said there was only one other alternative to staging the insider buyout with Geneen and the other investors: "Sit back and wait for Southern Pacific to find another buyer."

Unitog Company

"As far back as April, 1981, [Chairman Robert F.] Bob Hagans and [President] Arthur Brookfield had investigated the possibility of taking Unitog private. The idea of a private company, unhampered by excessive and costly government reporting requirements, and more flexible in meeting our customers' needs, sounded good!"

So read the lead article in Unitog's employee newsletter after the March, 1984, leveraged insider buyout for $36 million by a group of fifteen managers and a local venture capital group.

Unitog's business, with headquarters in Kansas City, Missouri, is the nationwide sales and rental of customized business and work uniforms and accessories to such clients as the U.S. Postal Service, Phillips 66, and Coca-Cola.

"We were tired of the public stock market, tired of the SEC [U.S. Securities and Exchange Commission] rules," Hagans said. "Now we are owned by employees.

"The shareholders loved it," he said of the "going private" buy-out. "They received a premium of forty percent over market price for a stock that had dawdled in the middle twenties for most of the past fifteen years."

Appendix

SELLER	BUYOUT COMPANY City Business
AGRICO CHEMICAL CO.	CROP PRODUCTION SERVICES Tulsa, OK *Retail fertilizer*
AKZONE'S ARMAK	AMERICAN TAPE Marysville, MI *Pressure-sensitive tapes*
ALLEGHENY BEVERAGE CORP.	ALLEGHENY PEPSI-COLA BOT- TLING CO. Baltimore, MD *Soft drinks*
ALLIED CORP.	AAC HOLDINGS Parsippany, NJ *Liquid fertilizers*
ALLIED CORP.	BORG TEXTILES Chicago, IL *Knit fibers*
ALLIED CORP.	CONVERSE, INC. Wilmington, MA *Sports shoes*
ALUMINUM CO. OF AMERICA (ALCOA)	ALCAS CUTLERY CORP. Olean, NY *Cutlery*
AMERICAN FINANCIAL CORP.	CHAMBERS BELT CO. Phoenix, AZ *Leather goods*
AMERICAN HOECHST	NYLON CORP. OF AMERICA Manchester, NH *Nylon-6 resins*
AMF	HARLEY-DAVIDSON MOTOR CO. Milwaukee, WI *Motorcycles*
AMF, INC.	ROADMASTER CORP. Olney, IL *Bikes, riding toys*
AMFAC, INC.	CAROLINA NURSERIES, INC. Moncks Corner, SC *Ornamental nursery plants*

AMFAC, INC.	GURNEY SEED AND NURSERY Yankton, SD *Mail-order seeds and garden products*
AMFAC, INC.	TRI-WEST, INC. San Mateo, CA *Turf, ground covers, nurseries*
ANDERSON INDUSTRIES, INC.	STANDARD-KNAPP, INC. Portland, CT *Automatic packaging machinery*
APPLIED MAGNETICS CORP.	KEY TECHNOLOGY CORP. Milton Freewater, OR *Electronic food-processing equipment*
AVON PRODUCTS, INC.	TIFFANY & CO. New York, NY *Retail jeweler*
BANDAG INC.	SHRADER'S, INC. Greenville, OH *Tire retreading, sales*
BANKRUPTCY COURT	McLOUTH STEEL PRODUCTS Detroit, MI *Steel*
BARNES ENGINEERING CO.	PHILA. BALL & ROLLER BEAR- INGS Philadelphia, PA *Manufacturing*
BASTIAN INDUSTRIES, INC.	BASTIAN INTERNATIONAL New York, NY *Food-service equipment*
BEATRICE COMPANIES	A-1 TOOLS Melrose Park, IL *Mold-making*
BEATRICE COMPANIES	MELNOR INDUSTRIES, INC. Moonachie, NJ *Lawn sprinklers*
BLACK & DECKER MFG. CO.	McCULLOUGH CORP. Los Angeles, CA *Gas chainsaws*
BROWN & SHARPE MFG. CO.	ROBOT SYSTEMS, INC. Norcross, GA *Robot systems*

BURLINGTON NORTHERN	EL PASO CHEMICAL Odessa, TX *Petrochemicals*
CABOT CORP., BOSTON	SUMMIT CORP. OF AMERICA Thomaston, CT *Electroplating outlet*
CHRIS-CRAFT INDUSTRIES	MURRAY CHRIS-CRAFT CRUIS- ERS Sarasota, FL *Boats*
CITIES SERVICE/OCCIDENTAL PETROLEUM	TENNESSEE CHEMICAL Atlanta, GA *Sulfuric acid, copper sulfate*
COOPER INDUSTRIES, INC.	AVIALL, INC. Dallas, TX *Service aircraft engines*
COOPER LABORATORIES, INC.	COOPER LASERSONICS Santa Clara, CA *Surgical products*
COOPER LABORATORIES, INC.	STERN METALS CO. Mount Vernon, NY *Precision dental metals*
CPC INTERNATIONAL, INC.	INFORMATION SCIENCE, INC. Montvale, NJ *Information systems*
DART & KRAFT	PLASTIC SPECIALTIES AND TECHNOLOGIES Rockaway, NJ *Plastic extrusions*
DIAMOND INTERNATIONAL	HEEKIN CAN, INC. Cincinnati, OH *Metal containers, aerosol cans*
DOW CHEMICAL/OSCAR MAYER	KARTRIDG PAK Davenport, IA *Food-processing machinery*
DUPONT CO.	VISTA CHEMICAL Houston, TX *PVC resins, surfactants*
ELECTRO-METHODS, INC.	BAUER/ELECTRO, INC. Farmington, CT *Aircraft-testing equipment*

FAMILY FOUNDERS	SUGARHOUSE MOTOR INN Middlebury, VT *Meals and lodging*
FAMILY FOUNDERS	GUILFORD INDUSTRIES Guilford, ME *Office furniture*
FAMILY FOUNDERS	HOUSE OF RONNIE New York, NY *Women's sportswear*
FAMILY FOUNDERS ESTATE	PEA SOUP ANDERSEN'S RES- TAURANTS Buellton, CA *Restaurants*
FAMILY: C. WILBUR PETERS	MINNESOTA FABRICS, INC. Charlotte, NC *Fabrics, curtains*
FIRST AMERICAN CORP., NASHVILLE	FIRST AMERICAN NATIONAL BANK OF TULLAHOMA Tullahoma, TN *Banking*
FISHER FOODS	DOMINICK'S FINER FOODS Northlake, IL *Supermarkets*
FMC	PT COMPONENTS Plants in seven states, Mexico, and Canada *Power transmission plants*
FOUNDER: CALVIN PAGE	G P TECHNOLOGIES, INC. Philadelphia, PA *Typewriter, printing parts*
FUQUA INDUSTRIES, INC.	MARTIN THEATRES CO. Columbus, GA *Theaters, TV, and radio broadcasting*
GANNETT COMPANY	OAKLAND TRIBUNE Oakland, CA *Newspaper*
GARDEN WAY, INC.	STOREY COMMUNICATIONS, INC. Pownal, VT *Book publishing*
GENERAL ELECTRIC CO.	LXD, INC. Beachwood, OH *Liquid crystal display*

GEOSOURCE, INC./AETNA LIFE	MOORCO INTERNATIONAL, INC. Houston, TX *Oil field engineering systems*
GIFFORD-HILL & CO.	METAL SALES MANUFACTURING Louisville, KY *Metal buildings and roofing*
GOULD, INC.	GNB BATTERIES Mendota Heights, IL *Lead-acid batteries*
GULF + WESTERN INDUSTRIES	CAPITAL INTERNATIONAL IN- SURANCE New York, NY *Insurance*
GULF + WESTERN INDUSTRIES	CONSOLIDATED CIGAR CO. Secaucus, NJ *Cigarmaker*
GULF + WESTERN INDUSTRIES	FAMOUS PLAYERS REALTY LTD. New York, NY *Real estate*
GULF + WESTERN INDUSTRIES	NEW JERSEY ZINC CO., THE New York, NY *Zinc chemicals*
GULF OIL	MILLMASTER ONYX GROUP, INC. New York, NY *Specialty chemicals*
HARRIS CORP.	HARRIS GRAPHICS CORP. Melbourne, FL *Printing*
HAZELTINE CORP.	ESPRIT SYSTEMS, INC. Melville, NY *Software, video displays*
HEUBLEIN, INC.	TEXAS CUSTOM BAKERS, INC. Dallas, TX *Baked goods*
HOUSEHOLD INTERNATIONAL	WIEN AIR ALASKA Anchorage, AK *Commercial airline*
INCO LIMITED	EXIDE CORP. Philadelphia, PA *Automotive batteries*

INCO LIMITED	EXIDE ELECTRONICS CORP. Philadelphia, PA *Power systems, emergency lights*
INCO LIMITED	RAYOVAC CORP. Madison, WI *Batteries, lighting devices*
INCO LIMITED	UNIVERSAL ELECTRIC CO. Owosso, MI *Heating, ventilating, and air conditioning*
INLAND STEEL CO.	GROTNES METALFORMING Chicago, IL *Metalforming systems*
INTERCOLE, INC.	BANNER METALS Stroudsburg, PA *Metal products, materials handling*
INTERNATIONAL GENERAL INDUSTRIES	AVIS INDUSTRIAL CORP. Upland, IN *Auto parts, electric generators*
INTERSTATE MOTOR FREIGHT SYSTEM	DIRECT TRANSPORTATION Downs View, ONT *Trucking*
KEMPER CORP.	KEMPER SPORTS MANAGEMENT Long Grove, IL *Sports activities*
KOPPERS CO., INC.	ENVIRONMENTAL ELEMENTS Baltimore, MD *Pollution controls*
KOPPERS CO., INC.	U.S. PLASTIC/CHEMICAL Putnam, CT *Polyester buttons*
LITTON INDUSTRIES, INC.	TECHNOGRAPHICS, INC. Fitchburg, MA *Paper, forms, printing*
LTV CORP.	INTEROCEAN STEAMSHIP CORP. New Orleans, LA *Shipping*
MANVILLE CORP.	JOHNS-MANVILLE CANADA, INC. Montreal, PQ *Asbestos products*

MARK CONTROLS CORP.	TRANSLOGIC CORP. Denver, CO *Indoor conveyances*
MAST INDUSTRIES, INC.	TUTTLEMAN & SON Bala Cynwyd, PA *Women's apparel*
MATTEL, INC.	RINGLING BROTHERS & BARNUM AND BAILEY Washington, DC *Circus*
MATTEL, INC.	WESTERN PUBLISHING CO. Racine, WI *Book publisher*
MEAD	COMPUCHEM Research Triangle, NC *Toxic-waste laboratory*
MEAD	GULF CONSOLIDATED SERVICES Houston, TX *Petrochemical equipment*
MONSANTO	EL DORADO CHEMICAL El Dorado, AR *Ammonium-nitrate fertilizer*
MORTON THIOKOL, INC.	SOUTHWEST CHEMICAL SERVICES, INC. Houston, TX *Polyolefin resins*
MacMILLAN, INC.	BRENTANO'S New York, NY *Retail books*
McKESSON CORP.	FOREMOST DAIRIES San Francisco, CA *Dairy products*
NATIONAL DISTILLERS	SEYMOUR BRASS TURNING CO. Seymour, CT *Brass wire, tubing*
NATIONAL STEEL	WEIRTON STEEL Weirton, WV *Steel*
NL INDUSTRIES	CASCHEM Bayonne, NJ *Castor-oil chemicals*

NORTON CO.	SIEBE NORTH, INC. Cranston, RI *Industrial safety products*
OCCIDENTAL CHEMICAL	RUCO POLYMER Hicksville, NY *Specialty polymers*
OCCIDENTAL PETROLEUM	OMI INTERNATIONAL Warren, MI *Metal finishing*
OLIN CORPORATION	U.S. REPEATING ARMS CO. New Haven, CT *Sporting arms*
OUTLET CO.	CHERRY WEBB & TOURAINE South Attleboro, MA *Specialty stores, women's apparel*
OWENS-ILLINOIS	LILY-TULIP Augusta, GA *Paper products*
PARTNERS	E & B MARINE, INC. Edison, NJ *Retail marine products*
PENN CENTRAL CORP.	ARVIDA CORP. Boca Raton, FL *Real estate development in GA, CA, FL*
PETROPLANE, INC.	STATER BROS. MARKETS Colton, CA *Supermarkets*
PHELPS-DODGE CORP.	CABLEC CORP. Yonkers, NY *Industrial cable*
PHILBRO-SALOMON, INC.	INTERCONTINENTAL DEVELOP- MENT New York, NY *Phosphates, fertilizer, oil, and gas*
PHILLIPS CHEMICAL CO.	INTERPLASTIC CORP. Minneapolis, MN *Polyester and vinyl resins*
PLESSEY, INC.	PRECISION SPECIALTY Los Angeles, CA *Cold-rolled stainless steel*

POPE, EVANS & ROBBINS, INC.	GIBRALTAR INDUSTRIES, INC. Brooklyn, NY *Dyeing, finishing*
PPG INDUSTRIES	LAUREL INDUSTRIES Pepper Pike, OH *Antimony oxide*
R. J. REYNOLDS INDUSTRIES	IDA-CAL FREIGHT LINES, INC. Nampa, ID *Trucking*
RAYMOND INDUSTRIES, INC.	SAFEWAY PRODUCTS, INC. Middletown, CT *Heating elements*
RAYTHEON CO.	MASTER SOFTWARE Watertown, MA *Computer software*
RCA	GIBSON GREETINGS Cincinnati, OH *Greeting cards*
REICHHOLD CHEMICALS, INC.	SEQUENTIA, INC. Strongsville, OH *Plastics*
ROBLIN INDUSTRIES, INC.	UNITED STEEL & WIRE CO. Battle Creek, MI *Shopping carts*
ROYAL PACKING INDUSTRIES	MADICO, INC. Woburn, MA *Window insulation*
SHAREHOLDERS*	ALBANY INTERNATIONAL Menands, NY *Papermaking fabrics*
SHAREHOLDERS	ARCATA CORP. San Francisco, CA *Forest products, printing, containers*
SHAREHOLDERS	B.C. CHRISTOPHER & CO. Kansas City, MO *Brokerage commodities, venture capital*
SHAREHOLDERS	BENCH CRAFT Blue Mountain, MS *Furniture*

*This category includes public companies that have been taken into the private sector.

SHAREHOLDERS	BEVERAGE MANAGEMENT Columbus, OH *Soft drinks*
SHAREHOLDERS	BLUE BELL, INC. Greensboro, NC *Wrangler blue jeans*
SHAREHOLDERS	BRODART CO. Williamsport, PA *School books, library products*
SHAREHOLDERS	BROOKS FASHION STORES, INC. New York, NY *Clothing stores*
SHAREHOLDERS	CANNON MILLS Kannapolis, NC *Household textiles*
SHAREHOLDERS	CCI CORP. Tulsa, OK *Oil equipment*
SHAREHOLDERS	CELLU-CRAFT, INC. New Hyde Park, NY *Protective food wrappings*
SHAREHOLDERS	COCA-COLA BOTTLING OF NEW YORK Greenwich, CT *Soft drinks*
SHAREHOLDERS	COCA-COLA BOTTLING OF MIAMI Miami, FL *Soft drinks*
SHAREHOLDERS	COMMONWEALTH THEATRES, INC. Kansas City, MO *Movies*
SHAREHOLDERS	CONE MILLS CORP. Greensboro, NC *Apparel fabric*
SHAREHOLDERS	CONGOLEUM CORP. Kearny, NJ *Flooring*
SHAREHOLDERS	COOK INTERNATIONAL, INC. Palm Beach, FL *Insurance, pest control*

SHAREHOLDERS	CUMMINGS, INC. Nashville, TN *Electric signs*
SHAREHOLDERS	DAN RIVER, INC. Danville, NC *Textiles*
SHAREHOLDERS	DENTSPLY INTERNATIONAL York, PA *Dental and optical supplies*
SHAREHOLDERS	DEVON GROUP, INC. New York, NY *Wine, spirits, publishing*
SHAREHOLDERS	DILLINGHAM CORP. San Francisco, CA *Tugboats, construction*
SHAREHOLDERS	DORCHESTER GAS CORP. Dallas, TX *Oil and gas exploration and refining*
SHAREHOLDERS	ELIXIR MERGER CORP. Gardena, CA *Recreational vehicle products*
SHAREHOLDERS	EMPIRE, INC. Lebanon, MO *Liquified petroleum gas*
SHAREHOLDERS	EMPIRE OF CAROLINA Deerfield Beach, FL *Toys, buttons, decorations*
SHAREHOLDERS	FABERGE, INC. New York, NY *Beauty products*
SHAREHOLDERS	FRED MEYER Portland, OR *Food retailer, distributor*
SHAREHOLDERS	GENERAL HOMES CONSOLIDATED Houston, TX *Residential builders*
SHAREHOLDERS	GOLDEN WEST TELEVISION Los Angeles, CA *KTLA-TV*

SHAREHOLDERS	GUARDIAN INDUSTRIES CORP. Northville, MI *Glass, building products*
SHAREHOLDERS	HARTE-HANKS COMMUNICA- TIONS San Antonio, TX *Newspapers, broadcasting*
SHAREHOLDERS	HOUDAILLE INDUSTRIES Fort Lauderdale, FL *Pumps, machine tools*
SHAREHOLDERS	INDUSTRIAL SALES CO. Baltimore, MD *Wire rope, cable*
SHAREHOLDERS	JONATHAN LOGAN, INC. Secaucus, NJ *Apparel*
SHAREHOLDERS	KANE-MILLER CORP. Tarrytown, NY *Food products*
SHAREHOLDERS	LEISURE & TECHNOLOGY CORP. Los Angeles, CA *Recreational vehicles*
SHAREHOLDERS	LIBERTY FABRICS OF N.Y. New York, NY *Lace netting, veils*
SHAREHOLDERS	MARLEY COMPANY, THE Mission Woods, KS *Cooling towers, water services*
SHAREHOLDERS	MEENAN OIL CO. Syosset, NY *Heating oil, oil and gas exploration*
SHAREHOLDERS	METROMEDIA, INC. New York, NY *Non-network broadcasting*
SHAREHOLDERS	MID-ATLANTIC COCA-COLA Silver Springs, MD *Soft drinks*
SHAREHOLDERS	MacANDREWS & FORBES GROUP New York, NY *Licorice and chocolate*

SHAREHOLDERS	NATIONAL MEDICAL CARE, INC. Waltham, MA *Home health care, dialysis*
SHAREHOLDERS	NFA CORP. Boston, MA *Fabrics, elastics*
SHAREHOLDERS	NIAGARA FRONTIER SERVICES Buffalo, NY *Supermarkets*
SHAREHOLDERS	NORRIS INDUSTRIES, INC. Long Beach, CA *Defense products*
SHAREHOLDERS	PANNILL KNITTING Martinsville, VA *Sweatshirts*
SHAREHOLDERS	PARSONS CORP. Pasadena, CA *Engineering and construction*
SHAREHOLDERS	PIECE GOODS SHOP CO. Winston-Salem, NC *Retail fabrics*
SHAREHOLDERS	QUESTOR CORP. Tampa, FL *Diversified manufacturing*
SHAREHOLDERS	RAYMOND INTERNATIONAL, INC. Houston, TX *Marine construction*
SHAREHOLDERS	REEVES BROTHERS, INC. New York, NY *Industrial foam and fabrics*
SHAREHOLDERS	SFN COMPANIES Glenview, IL *Publishing, communications*
SHAREHOLDERS	SIGNODE CORP. Glenview, IL *Steel, plastic strapping*
SHAREHOLDERS	STANDARD-COOSA-THATCHER Chattanooga, TN *Silk yarn and thread*

SHAREHOLDERS	TANNETICS, INC. Erie, PA *Refrigeration equipment*
SHAREHOLDERS	THOS. D. MURPHY CO. Red Oak, IA *Calendars*
SHAREHOLDERS	UNITOG CO. Kansas City, MO *Uniforms*
SHAREHOLDERS	VALLE'S STEAK HOUSE Wellesley, MA *Restaurants*
SHAREHOLDERS	VAUGHAN-JACKLIN CORP. Downers Grove, IL *Horticultural products*
SHAREHOLDERS	WACKENHUT CORP. Coral Gables, FL *Security, investigation*
SHAREHOLDERS	WILLIAMHOUSE-REGENCY New York, NY *Stationery*
SHAREHOLDERS	WOMETCO ENTERPRISES, INC. Miami, FL *Cable TV, Coca-Cola bottling*
SHAREHOLDERS and ESMARK	PUREX INDUSTRIES, INC. Lakewood, CA *Detergents, bleach*
SHORIN FAMILY DESCENDANT	TOPPS CHEWING GUM, INC. Brooklyn, NY *Bubble gum, confections*
SIGNAL COMPANIES	PULLMAN TRANSPORTATION CO. Princeton, NJ *Transportation equipment*
SINGER CO.	SNYDER GENERAL CORP. Dallas, TX *Heating and air conditioning*
SOUTHERN PACIFIC CO.	TICOR Los Angeles, CA *Title insurance*

SPERRY CORP.	REMINGTON PRODUCTS, INC. Bridgeport, CT *Electric shavers*
SQUIBB	COIL PRODUCTS New Brunswick, NJ *Fermentation chemicals*
STORER COMMUNICATIONS, INC.	STORER CABLE COMMUNICA- TIONS OF PRINCE GEORGE'S COUNTY, MARYLAND Greenbelt, MD *Cable TV*
SUN CO.	SUN DATA Wayne, PA *Data processing*
TAFT BROADCASTING CO.	KINGS ENTERTAINMENT CO. Kings Island, OH *Theme parks*
TELECO, INC.	WTTV-TV Bloomington, IN *Television station*
TENNECO CORP.	NUODEX, INC. Piscataway, NJ *Specialty chemicals*
THE CONTINENTAL GROUP, INC.	TEEPAK, INC. Chicago, IL *Meat casings*
THE LIMITED, INC.	COWARD SHOE, INC. New York, NY *Shoe stores*
TIMES MIRROR CO.	NEW AMERICAN LIBRARY New York, NY *Publishing*
TRACOR, INC.	TRACOR ANALYTIC, INC. Elk Grove, IL *Biomedical products*
U.S. STEEL CORP.	McDONALD STEEL CORP. Youngstown, OH *Steel*
U.S. STEEL CORP.	JOHNSTOWN CORP. Johnstown, PA *Steel*

VULCAN, INC.	CHEMUNG FOUNDRY CORP. Elmira, NY *Castings, gear housings*
VULCAN, INC.	VULCAN ENGINEERING CO. Pittsburgh, PA *Engineering services*
VULCAN, INC.	WESTMORELAND PLASTICS Latrobe, PA *Injection and molded plastic*
W. R. GRACE	CHEMED Cincinnati, OH *Laundry chemicals*
WANG LABORATORIES, INC.	GENESYS SOFTWARE SYSTEMS Lawrence, MA *Computer software*
WHITTAKER CORP.	WHITTAKER MEDICUS Evanston, IL *Health care services*
ZAPATA CORP.	STANFORD COAL CO. Lexington, KY *Coal mining*
ZIFF-DAVIS PUBLISHING CO.	RALPH E. BECKER AND PARTNERS New York, NY *Television stations*

Index